LESSONS *from*
HISTORY

LESSONS *from*
HISTORY

PART 1

WADIH T. BARAKAT

LESSONS FROM HISTORY

iUniverse books may be ordered through booksellers or by contacting:

iUniverse
1663 Liberty Drive
Bloomington, IN 47403
www.iuniverse.com
844-349-9409

Because of the dynamic nature of the Internet, any web addresses or links contained in this book may have changed since publication and may no longer be valid. The views expressed in this work are solely those of the author and do not necessarily reflect the views of the publisher, and the publisher hereby disclaims any responsibility for them.

Any people depicted in stock imagery provided by Getty Images are models, and such images are being used for illustrative purposes only. Certain stock imagery © Getty Images.

ISBN: 978-1-6632-2243-5 (sc)
ISBN: 978-1-6632-2244-2 (e)

Print information available on the last page.

iUniverse rev. date: 05/07/2021

DEDICATION

TO:

The spirit of my mother VIOLETTE whose love is still burning inside me.

The spirit of my father TANNOUS whose lucidity is still giving me hope.

The spirit of my sister NOHAD whose devotion to reading made me a book worm.

The spirit of ROBERT S. FRANGIEH who taught me war and peace.

TO:

My wife HOUDA with all the love that she deserves for the endless support.

My son PETER who always encouraged me to finish this work carefully.

My brother BADOUI hoping this book can fill a bit of my absence in his life.

My friend TANNOUS who helped me by his continuous "BRAVO".

All my students in *College De La Salle,* especially those we had with them acute conversations and debates.

PROLOGUE

People who are not keen to read history are predestined to live it again with its pros and cons.

Lots of different schools are associated with writing history, still all of them agree on one principle, it is the necessity to learn from history, regardless whether the history is biased or not. Here dwells the knowledge of reading history.

Lots of histories were written, still we need to write more. For the more we need to know about the present is equal to the more we need to know about the past. Consequently, the nearer we will be to undertake the future.

Lots of historians wrote different history books. Some measured and weighed wars, some others peace. But in both cases historians are the only shareholders of history itself, because they had read, they had questioned and provided answers even if those answers are not adequate to some of us; they are still essential lessons.

Every walk of life has its historians, as every historian has his own angle of vision to this very walk of life. So what we should do is to be selective in our choice. Our choice has to be like the terrace in which we must seed the grain for a better crop. If one plants his apple tree in the lower terrace, this apple tree will have its water and the water filtering in the ground from the upper terraces and the apple fruits will not have the delicious taste that has to have naturally.

Nature in its charms does not like void. That means, if I do not read history, another is going to read it, and have and be what I am supposed to have and be.

Fortunate is the teacher who can teach his students to read and question history, for history is the only provider of the truth of our present. Pity is the student who does not have such a teacher.

What your eyes are going to meet is not only a copy-paste work, but also an in-depth look of my own interest and assumption of what may fit all the minds and the situations we are going through nowadays. On one hand, some extracts might be of interest to statesmen, but in their turn might be of interest to the public so they will better understand the statesmen of today. On the other hand, some citations are put here for the statesmen to better understand the public.

Finally, I would like to say the following to the reader: "Thank you for being patient my dear reader, because you will see the self-reflection within what lies in this volume."

By the author

CHAPTER 1

OUR ORIENTAL HERITAGE. VOL 1

The Economic Elements of Civilization

1. Rights do not come to us from nature, which knows no rights except cunning and strength; they are privileges to individuals by the community as advantageous to the common good. Liberty is a luxury of security; the free individual is a product and a mark of civilization. (p.29)

    Reflection: Rights are often confused with freedom. Nature leaves no place for delicate confusions if we look enough thoroughly into it.

2. Women pitch our tents, make our clothes, and keep us warm at night... (p.33)

    Reflection: From a different perspective, the real woman keeps you busy all day long.

The moral Elements of Civilization

3. As Beaumarchais put it, man differs from the animal in eating without being hungry, drinking without being thirsty, and making love at all seasons. (p.45)

Reflection: From the point of view of Beaumarchais, he was right for he had seen that in the middle of the eighteenth century. But the fact is also subject to change, so nowadays we may differ with him.

4. Individualism, like liberty, is a luxury of civilization. (p.51)

Reflection: Because it is very true that a civilization, in order to be grown up, it must follow the moto of the famous three musketeers: "One for all and all for one." Once this relation is broken, the civilization is doomed to decay.

5. Every vice was once a virtue, necessary for the struggle of existence; it became a vice only when it survived the conditions that made it indispensable; a vice, therefore, is not

3

an advanced form of behavior, but usually an atavistic (primitive) throwback to ancient and superseded (archaic) ways. It is one purpose of a moral code to adjust the unchanged –or slowly changing–impulses of human nature to the changing needs and circumstances of social life. (p.51)

Reflection: Since everything is subject to change, and since the change itself is continuous, all what we can do is to use this golden chance to make the change as fruitful and positive as possible. Still the question goes around whether this fruitfulness is individual or general. By this we can conclude that the nature of the change of any deed or any idea is equivocal.

6. In general, dishonesty rises with civilization, because under civilization the stakes (risks) of diplomacy are larger, there are more things to be stolen, and education makes men clever. When property develops among primitive men, lying and stealing come in its strain. (p.52)

Reflection: Every development brings along with what is necessary some unnecessary concepts. This is why we must try to be as eclectic as we can in order to reduce the secondary damages that are to take place due to the adjacent extras.

7. Where food is dear life is cheap. (p.53)

Reflection: Survival is a key issue in defining the value of every walk of life. According to Abraham Maslow the basis of survival has always started with food provision to feel secure.

8. Worship, if not the child, is at least the brother of fear. (p.63)

Reflection: Human being has always categorized the unknown or the unconceived as superpower. Thus, this unknown has constantly created fear. In one hand, fear weakens the self-esteem, on the other, it provides determination to invent or create a new understanding to this mystery so the human can bridle it and bring it under his control.

The Mental Elements of civilization

9. Has any other invention ever equaled, in power and glory, the common noun? (p.75)

   Reflection: Identification is still the only way to correctly describe anything, any one or any idea; to do so we must make this more common. Therefore, we have to keep on inventing common nouns which are more and more adequate to describe a given thing, person or idea correctly for the sake of the unbiased usage of any language.

10. Civilization is an accumulation, a treasure-house of arts and wisdom, manners and morals, from which the individual, in his development, draws nourishment for his mental life; without that periodical reacquisition of the racial heritage by each generation, civilization would die a sudden death. It owes its life to education. (p.74)

    Reflection: In case we neglect the educational curricula, and in case we don't include in them the inherited treasures that are the product of all the advantageous and historical experiments, surely the civilization is threatened. Consequently, the safe and sound inheritance must be transmitted correctly to help improve the human race.

11. The primitive father put his trust in character, as modern education has put its trust in intellect; he was concerned to make not scholars but men. (p.75)

   Reflection: The absence of a wise selection will certainly lead to a poor product. Strangely, when the burden of education was on the shoulder of the father of the family, the product of characters was more human; when it became the responsibility of a system it became more careless.

12. Beauty is any quality by which an object or a form pleases a beholder. Primarily and originally the object does not please the beholder because it is beautiful, but rather he calls it beautiful because it pleases him. (p.82)

Reflection: Though some believes that beauty does exist without being seen and without being distinguished, still the beauty needs to be certified as beauty by the beholder himself. Otherwise, it cannot affect anyone and it remains dying unless it is discovered.

13. Art is the creation of beauty; it is the expression of thought or feeling in a form that seems beautiful or sublime, and therefore arouses in us some reverberation (echo) of that primordial delight which woman gives to man, or man to woman. (p.83)

Reflection: Any work of art raises to prove beauty in its sublime state. It must have the seed of creation to express outstandingly a certain message and carry within itself an abundance of a given beauty.

14. From these many sources come those noble superfluities of life–the arts even philosophy. For what is philosophy but an art to give "significant form" to the chaos of experience? (p.83)

Reflection: The historian (Will Durant) here emphasizes on the following sources: thought, feeling, form and even color within a form. And as a result to the presence of some or all these sources arts and philosophies sprout to flourish and create chains of reactions in the individuals, in societies or in cultures which we name them later experiences.

15. If the sense of beauty is not strong in primitive society, it may be because the lack of delay between sexual desire and fulfillment gives no time for that imaginative enhancement of the object which makes so much of the object's beauty. (p.83)

Reflection: We still experience this delay and its consequences in our days and for sure we will do the same for the coming future. This is a normal development in human nature that could not be found normally in animal nature. Thus, beauty is taking more forms to humans because humans can discover the forms of beauty automatically with each inch of their progress.

Sumeria

16. Surely there is nothing new under the sun; and the difference between the first woman and the last could pass through the eye of a needle. (p.130)

Reflection: *Though this is very subjective, but we still have the chance to see it among some sexual concepts. Unfortunately, this notion, in some cultures, finds its suitable environment to propagate very easily.*

Egypt

17. It is evident that nature had long since learned how to make men, and art had long since learned how to represent them. (p.148)

Reflection: *Everything that is aesthetically or artistically displayed is attractive to some people. Moreover, the nature-made work, especially men, takes generations to be accomplished. Thus, its striking level is much higher than any man-made. Taking into consideration the precedent quote and reflection # 15.*

Babylonia

18. It is almost a law of history that the same wealth that generates a civilization announces its decay. (p.222)

    Reflection: It is not only the law of history, but also it is the law of nature. Because the wealth itself that brings any culture up to take its real place on the line of history, this very wealth comes to be innate and forgotten; thus, mismanaged. Consequently, it starts to dictate the fate of its offspring, the civilization.

19. Love, stronger than death, is restored to its rightful place as master of gods and men. (p.239)

    Reflection: Love still throughout all times proves to be the strongest and the most endurable policy that man can have. Love needs not to be restored to any place because it is always in its rightful place. Loves choses to be naturally where to be and never was it chosen. Wherever love dwells, it is and exists. Not only love does it master gods and men, but also the entire mother nature as her sole and loyal spouse.

20. Morals grew lax when the temples grew rich. (p.248)

Reflection: It is the negative effect of being rich. When a nation needs more financial security, it strives to secure it. When it secures the desirable financial security, it forgets how necessary it was to secure it, and by this its way down starts. The longer the nation forgets about how important this security, the nearer it comes to its decay.

21. Reconstruction of the whole from a part is hazardous in history, and writing history is the reconstruction of the whole from a part. (p.259)

Reflection: Usually any construction of an entity starts from a special part which is the basis. However, in history, the reconstruction is reversed. In order to write a historical episode, one has to have the true bulk of this very same occasion if possible. In case it is very hard to seize it correctly, all the historical reconstruction will take an off course penchant. As a result, the target will be lost, and this episode will be incorrect. Finally, here lies the jeopardy of writing history.

22. A nation is born stoic (enduring), and dies epicurean (pleasure-loving). (p. 259)

Reflection: A nation is like a man; the first years of the man's life is surrounded by all the means of protection in order to endure the diseases. The time the man starts to become independent, more dangers are to encounter him. Meanwhile he becomes more and more life-loving. The more life-loving he becomes, the nearer he gets to his inescapable fate, the death.

23. Evil does not destroy faith, but strengthens it. (p.259)

Reflection: "Where sin abounded, grace abounded", St Paul. Very simple. One has to have faith first, then, when evil comes, it strengthens it. Because faith is always rightful. And righteousness reigns in the end.

24. If victory comes, if war is forgotten in security and peace, then wealth grows; the life of the body gives way, in the dominant classes, to the life of the senses and the mind; toil and suffering are replaced by pleasure and ease; science weakens faith even while thought and comfort weaken virility and fortitude (courage). (p.259)

Reflection: It is the same vicious cycle. The ecstasy of victory more often leads to forget the hardships exercised to achieve this victory. And here lies the precise seed of weakness. Here comes the turn of the richness to grow in a peaceful and secure environment. The unaware nation sinks deeper in the lax abysses of senses and emotions and it becomes even weaker for it will not consider the importance of the readiness to the unwillingly neglected coming troubles. The dominance of the life of pleasures wanes on the sake of the lack of mindfulness. Then the balance of equilibrium starts to tend towards cowardice and immorality. To end, the cycle close by the

destruction of the waning culture and the rise of
a new stoic one. (refer to quote # 22)

Assyria

25. War was often more profitable than peace; it cemented discipline, intensified patriotism, strengthened the royal power. (p.272)

   Reflection: In addition to all these benefits, war filters societies to the maximum: all the invalids or the useless for the survival of the nation will be rejected and expelled from the gain sharing and later from responsibilities. And the eligible will take more responsibilities and more gains till their turn comes and be thrown out.

26. In each victory it was the strongest and bravest who died, while the infirm and cautious to multiply their kind; it was a dysgenic (defective to the hereditary qualities) process that perhaps made for civilization by weeding out(clearing) the more brutal types, but undermined the biological basis upon which Assyria had risen to power. (p.283)

Reflection: We come to encounter here a strong counter idea to the previous one. Victories or defeats are the only results to wars; however; the analysts argue that the strength and bravery are not compulsory criteria to the wise person. Though this brave has always had his role to die or to kill. As the cautious and infirm have always had their roles to multiply due the higher level of intelligence they have to secure the win in the survival game of humans. Thus, the trace of human is always crescendo.

Judea

27. Since the flesh was weak and the Law complex, sin was inevitable. (p.313)

Reflection: The complexity by which all the laws were created and are still sustained, though they are subject to change, charges us a very high price as humans. This price we have to pay while we are practicing the laws we put to hinder the development of the vice over virtue. However, the weakness which we inherit and the tendency towards the ease which we enjoy, make the inevitability to sin continuous. Here lies the seed of the eternal conflict between the good and the bad. Consequently, no law is sublime.

28. Poverty is created by wealth and never knows itself poor until riches stare it in the face. (p. 314)

Reflection: Envy and fear are the energizers of poverty and wealth. Envy feeds the hearts of poor and fear the hearts of wealthy. If a poor person has the heart clean, he will never feel the envy that keeps him poor. As well, if a wealthy person does not have the fear of being poor and losing his wealth, his heart will always be clean. In this case, both are equal.

29. Both the serpent and the fig were probably phallic symbols (symbol of the male organ); behind the myth is the thought that sex and knowledge destroy innocence and happiness; and are the origin of evil. (p. 329)

Reflection: *Any excess in both sex and knowledge is destructing to the ones who are not apt to hold that much of it. The extra in anything undoubtedly causes disequilibrium then conflicts. Here comes the war in its concept in the quote # 25 to bring back the equilibrium.*

30. Even a fool when he holds his peace is counted wise. (p.343)

Reflection: *Even a fool can wisely prove that silence is much more precious than words. Like this, everybody can put himself on the safe side. Moreover, one character of a wise man is to speak less and listen more.*

31. A noble book; all men's book. (p.343)

Reflection: *Normally a book is the best man's friend. What if the book is a noble one? Nobility is a rare character nowadays; it is what raises the man from a certain standard to a higher one. Though it is rare; it remains reachable. This decent charm has always proved to be invincible and every one longs to possess. The lowest of man seeks to be noble or even dreams of being.*

32.   The sleep of a laboring man is sweet, whether he eats little or much; but the abundance of the rich will not suffer him to sleep. (p.347)

Reflection: The fatigue of the body is quickly washable, but that of the mind is very exhausting. It has never been a question of poor or rich man, both can have dignity and goodness in order to avoid pain caused by cruelty and misdeeds. The abundance of food can not hinder the sweet sleep and the clear conscience.

33.   Even wisdom is a questionable thing; anything more than a little knowledge is a dangerous thing. (p.348)

Reflection: A donkey with full load of gold is still a donkey with full load of gold. It can never be a wise or a rich donkey. In contrast, a man with little wisdom is undoubtedly a wise man. However, all is relative. Even a little learning is a dangerous thing, because a learned man can turn intoxicated and be of a great danger to his community.

34. Wisdom is good; with an inheritance; otherwise it is a snare (trap), and is apt to destroy its lovers. (p.348)

   Reflection: Wisdom can never be inherited. It has always been the sum of knowledge and experience with an inherited character of readiness. Altogether can produce a wise man. Otherwise, this so-called wisdom will be fake and sooner or later will be revealed to other perceiving persons.

35. In much wisdom is much grief; and he that increases knowledge increases sorrow. (p.348)

   Reflection: The wiser a man is, the more burdens are on his shoulders. The man who becomes richer or wiser is the man who has to understand and tolerate himself and the others. Beware, the higher a man is on the scale of his society, the harder his fall will be.

Persia

36. It is the fatality of empire to breed repeated war. For the conquered must be periodically re-conquered. In such situation wars must be invented if they do not arise of their own accord. (p.355)

Reflection: *Repeated wars is almost a normal cycle in a nation though the results are not always up to the expectations. But what often proved to be an obligation is the re-making of wars so that the strong remains strong and the weak stays weak. Some states are made only to have wars on their territories because other states have to invent them.*

37. Humanity loves poetry more than logic, and without a myth the people perish. (p.371)

Reflection: *It has always been favored to have things as easy as possible. Poetry is easier to be written than some lines on the history face which needs more logic than dream. However, imagination can go farther and quicker than reality. Likewise, all kinds of logics start as ideas in the very beginning.*

38. It would be unfair to judge the people from their kings; virtue is not news, and virtuous men, like happy nations, have no history. (p.373)

Reflection: As men can make kings; kings can make nations. If a king senses what his subjects need or are, he reflects what they are. Rare are these situations through history when a supreme is virtuous, he sows virtues among the people and the whole nation will be virtuous; thus, virtue becomes reality and not only news. When the virtue is like thorn in the king's flesh, then virtue is daily news.

39. There was never yet a handsome man who was not vain, nor any physically vain main whom some woman has not led by the nose. (p.381)

Reflection: Mostly often it is a package in which beauty and unproductivity come in. Consequently, when beauty comes along with strength, intelligence and usefulness, a man here is a rare piece of God's work, for he is neither to be held by his nose, nor he accepts to hold others by their noses.

India

40. Our knowledge of the past is an occasional gap in our ignorance. (p.396)

Reflection: History is full of holes. No historian can write a perfect history, for nothing is perfect. Ignorance is what lacks in the puzzle of our knowledge, for this reason, nobody's knowledge is complete. The more one can gather data, the more he will witness breaches in what he knows. Still the curiosity to know is the only cure to fill the gaps in the collective knowledge.

41. Forever the north produces rulers and warriors, the south produces artists and saints, and the meek inherits heaven. (p.397)

Reflection: This theory of the reigning north lives in minds of many sociologists for long times, but now, due to the mixing of cultures, such a theory can no longer exist as strong as it has once been. Many examples can be seen nowadays that contradict or reverse this old theory. Rulers and warriors are not anymore the exclusiveness to the north, as well, artists and saints are never the specificity of the south. So all can inherit heaven.

42. Life is pain, that pain is due to desire, and wisdom lies in stilling all desire. (p.429)

Reflection: Life is mostly painful. Yes. Because everybody desires a comfortable life and as easy as possible, and this comfort usually comes on the account of others. As the famous proverb says:" one man's meat is another man's poison." There is a kind of cunning men who name wisdom the art of stealing the desire of others.

Refer to quote # 1

43. The eternal vigilance is the price of civilization. A nation must love peace, but keep its powder dry. (p.463)

Reflection: A Roman general once said:" If you want peace, prepare for war." It is a very high price a nation must pay to keep itself away from dangers. This also implies on individuals to keep themselves on the safe side.

44. The strength of the ruler is often the weakness of his government. (p.466)

Reflection: Whenever the people are weak, the ruler has to maintain his state by having a certain tendency to be a tyrant. Or reciprocally, the tyrant weakens his people to maintain his tyranny. An equilibrium must take place even if it is unjust.

45. The superiority of man rests on the jewels of reason. (p. 469)

Reflection: Since man is the only creature who has a reasonable sense of reason, and since he has the gift to promote and to use this reason for his advancement, his superiority keeps governing over all other creatures.

46. He took the rotundity (marked with fullness and cadence) of the moon, and the curves of creepers, and the clinging (sticking) of tendrils, and the trembling of the grass, and the slenderness (fineness)of the reed (arrow), and the bloom of flowers, and the lightness of the leaves, and the tapering (narrowing) of the elephant's trunk, and the glances of deer, and the clustering of rows of bees, and the joyous gaiety of sunbeams, and the weeping of clouds, and the fickleness (uncertainty) of the winds, and the timidity of the hare, and the vanity (pride) of the peacock, and the softness of the parrot's bosom, and the hardness of adamant (diamond), and the sweetness of honey, and the cruelty of the tiger, and the warm of glow of fire, and the coldness of snow, and the chattering of jays, and the cooing of *kokila*, and the hypocrisy of the crane, and the fidelity of the *chakravaka*; and compounding all these together he made woman, and gave her to man. (p. 429)

Reflection: And gave her to man.... She is so sweet that we, men, cannot digest her without the shock of disturbance in case we want to take all of these characters that God dripped in her. After all, we are very grateful, for, in my opinion, we balance each other.

47. When a woman is merely a woman – when she winds herself round and round men's heart with her smiles and sobs and services and caressing endearments – then she is happy. (p. 493)

   Reflection: By completing his job, every man feels satisfied. What if the job is to satisfy the others by performing the dearest of the deeds to him, then the outcome will be doubled! A woman can be a mother, a sister, a wife, a daughter, or even sometimes a mistress. Whoever she is, she fills in the gaps, she bridges and she soothes.

48. Every people harbors all virtues and vices. (p. 499)

   Reflection: The intimate historical twins are vice and virtues. Each necessitates the existence of the other. One cannot live all his days in white;

he will be snow blinded. As well, one cannot live in total darkness; he will be sightless.

49. Life is a stage with one entrance but many exits. (p. 502)

Reflection: Everybody knows when, where and how he was born. But no one can tell when, where and how he will die.

50. The real problem of life is not suffering but undeserved suffering. (p. 516)

Reflection: This is what we call it cruelty. Whatever one may experience, he can apprehend in his own heart whether he deserves his reward or his punishment.

51. Heat cannot understand cold. (p. 516)

Reflection: And so cold cannot understand heat, for they are in the same time the eternal enemies and the eternal correlatives. One is the cause to the other. As Leo Tolstoy put it:" Russia and summer never mix."

52. Humanity doubts its gods most when it prospers, and worships them most when it is miserable. (p. 522)

Reflection: The need to ask for a help does exist only when we really need help. In particular, in old times when man used to know little on God or gods. It is the fear of losing the causes or motivations to survive.

53. There is no humorist like history. (p. 525)

Reflection: An impartial history almost always touches the strings of sensibility in the man's mind. It stirs in him either mockery or homage. And because there is no perfect history, we can conclude that history always brings along with her satire.

54. The student needs not the logic of reason so much as a cleansing and deepening discipline of the soul. This, perhaps, has been the secret of all profound education. (p .547)

Reflection: As an experienced educator, I strongly agree with Will Durant here. The soul, in education, is the recipient which will hold all the data spilt in it because it is the artefact of what the society provides along with all the inherited types which will force the reason to act in a finite way. Imagine you put the wine in a barrel of the finest wood or you put it in a metal barrel. And the result will definitely be dissimilar.

55. Virtue is not the quiet heroism of good works, nor any pious ecstasy; it is simply the recognition of the identity of the self with every other self. (p. 553)

Reflection: Virtue has never been a piece of work or any like. It has never been a feeling of good deeds. Virtue is the rare supremacy of self-giving for the sake of the other in order to let this other feel supreme. And here lies the real peril.

56. Empty notions and mere fancies are very hard to understand and very easy to forget. (p. 560)

Reflection: This is because what lasts is only the work we leave behind us, whatever its consequence is. One will always be remembered for his deeds not for his dreams.

57. How little do they know who speak of us with censure? The entertainment is not for them. Possibly someone exists or will exist, of similar taste with myself; for time is boundless, and the world is wide. (p. 576)

Reflection: Never look behind you. If you believe in the righteousness of your conducts, "all you need to say is simply 'Yes' or 'No'; anything beyond this comes from the evil. "Matthew 37:5

58. I have taken refuge at your feet, my beloved. When I do not see you, my mind has no rest... I cannot forget your grace and your charm, and yet there is no desire in my heart. (p. 581) Indian Brahman "Chandi Das"

Reflection: In the Psalm 91:2 it is written:" My refuge and my fortress, my God, in whom I trust." The year was around 1015 B.C. In the 11ᵗʰ century A.D, this Indian Brahman wrote his quote to someone he loved and was excommunicated by his fellow Brahmans. This proves the saying of Matthew in the previous Quote.

59. The profoundest beauty of woman may be more in motherhood than in youth, more in Demeter than in Aphrodite, and more in my mother than in my girlfriend.(p. 595)

Reflection: For the beauty to attain its zenith, it must be turned to be a virtue and let the inside reflect to the outside. Real motherhood is one of the extreme self-giving states. It is incarnated in the whole being, not only from the inside but also to the outside. My mother is by all means the most beautiful woman God ever created if I can perceive this and if she is performing her job correctly. The more I contemplate her sacrifices, the deeper I reach to her perfect beauty.

60. A people that has lost the ability to govern itself, or to develop its natural resources, inevitably falls a prey to nations suffering from strength and greed. (p. 614)

Reflection: It is nature's law that the greedy and the fittest dominates the lazy and the weak. The prey makes itself a prey by showing its weakness point, whether willingly or naturally, to the predator. And normally the predator pushed by its strength and greed starts the chase. The same law is adopted by the nations. It is the survival instinct applied to men and nations equally.

61. The knowledge of God may be likened to a man, while love of God is like a woman. Knowledge has entry only to the outer rooms of God, and no one can enter into the inner mysteries of God save a lover. (p. 617)

Reflection: In the first letter of St. John, he chooses the virtue of love above all virtues. If we perceive deeply in the scriptures of the most lasting religions in history, we find that love stands above and it is always the most difficult to possess and the most influential. In conclusion, it is easy to attain one's heart by love, but never by any other virtue or fortune. The heart of God is the most sacred home for humans, it is the Holy of Holies, it is the nucleus where all other virtues starts and stays intact. As long as the woman represents the soft and tender side of humanity, so she is the agent who stirs in us, as humans, the highest level of the sense of love. Throughout history the woman represents the virginity, the tenderness, the purity and the love. We can count many of them.

62. To be converted from one religion to another is foolishness; one needs only to continue his own way, and reach the essence of his own faith. All rivers flow to the ocean. (p. 617)

Reflection: To the atheists, this quote means nothing to them. To the polytheists, it is very profitable to shift from one belief to another. However, the monotheists are very much in solidarities with one God; therefore, one religion. Still we can find some monotheists who prefer to convert their religion for substantial gains. They cannot be counted believers. Some others are being converted for they either don't have the strong belief that this religion will take them to salvation, or they find in another religion the sanctuary to their minds and their whole being.

63. The highest truth is this:" God is present in all beings. They are His multiple forms. There is no other God to seek. He alone serves God who serves all other beings". (p. 618)

Reflection: If we look deeply into the verb "serve" in this quote, we can consider it as the verb "love" in the Holy Bible. To serve somebody needs sacrifice and dignity. A real servant is the one who can sacrifice and give away what he needs to let the others feel safe or even safer. The parents diligently sacrifice for the sake of their children's happiness. Some sisters, some brothers and some real lovers, too do the same thing. They do this for they do believe that their deeds make them nearer to God Himself. What if you serve those who they are not of your kin? Let's have a look on this quote from the movie "Maid in Manhattan": (To serve people takes dignity and intelligence. But remember, they are only people with money. And although we serve them, we are not their servants. What we do does not define who we are. What defines us is how well we rise after falling.)

64. Nature, though sometimes terrible, is always sublime, never bleak, or barren, or hideous. (p. 620)

Reflection: The mother nature is really the good example of a perfect mother. Though sometimes our mothers are very directive with us, they do so for our own benefits. We almost always do not understand them on the spot but we finally got the insight and especially when we will not be able to show them gratitude. All the elements of nature are necessary for the continuity of all the normal cycles that let us live and prosper. We cannot see the fruitfulness of a terrible natural incident because we are focusing on our own benefits which blind us from the profitability of its output to the whole community. Here lies the core selfishness and the aloofness of the individual.

65. When I go from hence let this be my parting word, that what I have seen is unsurpassable. "Tagore" (p. 620)

Reflection: It is the contentment of one's person by the fortune that he had found his lover and he had lived with her or him for the rest of his life as the most loveable person in history. Every one of us can say this quote defining how lucky he was with his wife or husband.

66. They all have need of me, and I have no time to brood over the after-life. I am of an age with each; what matter if my hair turns grey?" Tagore" (p. 621)

Reflection: Unaging is unnatural. What you cannot solve when alive can be solved when you are not, in case you can leave behind you the key to the previewed issues to come. Sometimes we hear from our grandfathers a story that may mean nothing to us, but with time that very story will help us solve very complicated problems.

67. What the eyes are for the outer world, fasts are for the inner." Gandhi" (p. 627)

   Reflection: Temptation is a major interrogation in one's life. All what is right or wrong comes as a result of one's definition of temptation. The eye shows us the outer world and then we are led into temptation; the desire to have is an inner temptation. Whatever the desire is, it may lead us to be doomed if not controlled.

68. History teaches those who have, no doubt with honest motives, ousted the greedy by using brute force against them; have in their turn become preys to the disease of the conquered. My interest in India's freedom will cease if she adopts violent means. For their fruit will be not freedom, but slavery." Gandhi" (p. 631)

   Reflection: It is better to try to tame the beast than to try to kill him. The greedy person is a person who adopts the greed as a way to prove himself in his neighboring as he finds it an easy way to follow. Still it is more valuable to train himself for hardships in order to accomplish more durable deeds which history can assimilate for longer periods and then he will be nearly immortal. Gandhi was so ambitious to put India on this trajectory.

69. It was Gandhi's task to unify India; and he accomplished it. Other tasks await other men. (p. 632)

Reflection: Most of the history makers agree that not all of their dreams can be achieved in one span's life. They always prepare to others to complete what they have already started. Because they do believe that priority setting comes prior to priority accomplishing.

70. India will teach us the tolerance and gentleness of the mature mind, the quiet content of the un-acquisitive soul, the calm of the understanding spirit, and a unifying, pacifying love for all living things. (p. 633)

Reflection: Without any exceptions, indeed all living things are respected in the Indian mythologies. According to the Indians beliefs, each and every living thing has its rank and it has its role to be played in the commotion of the lives lived there.

China

71. He was kind and benevolent as Heaven, wise and discerning as the gods. From afar his radiance was like a shining cloud, and approaching near him he was as brilliant as the sun. Rich was he without ostentation, and regal without luxuriousness. (p.643)

Reflection: Here Will Durant is repeating the words of "The Book of History" which mentions the great events in the legendary history of China. Although the words are very idealistic and far from our present, we can still breathe from them the very essence that we lack today. All the attributes we read in this quote, that depicting Yao, the great ruler of China, are really mystical but very inspirational.

72. In the end the two hostile forces, custom and law, arrived at a wholesome compromise: the reach

of law was narrowed to major or national issues, while the force of custom continued in all minor matters; and since human affairs are mostly minor matters, custom remained king. (p.646)

Reflection: *Custom and law, the twin eternal foes, if they don't reach any compromise, there would have never been any culture at all. Because cultures need a certain set of laws in order to be able to grow and live, laws are obliged to find what suits the people to exist. Thus, the only way for laws to be generated is to find their inspiring mechanism which is undoubtedly the customs. Peoples get accustomed to what fits them to survive, and this is what is called traditions which protect and made their heritage and root them to their territories. However, the dispute on whether the laws or customs come first and are the most important is everlasting. As long as there are laws need to be renewed, I think the reference should lean on customs.*

73. Knowledge is not virtue; on the contrary, rascals have increased since education spread. Knowledge is not wisdom, for nothing is so

far from a sage as an "intellectual". They damage every natural process with theory; their ability to make speeches and multiply ideas is precisely the sign of their incapacity for action. (p.653)

Reflection: Knowledge is a huge responsibility. It is a pressing burden that wears out the person and brings him to be a wise guy rather than a wise man. A wise man is a successful student of life who can turn every failure to a happy moment but not necessarily to a full success. Education, if not placed in its right place and time, it may become a very dangerous weapon. Yet wisdom can come earlier than its right time and place. For this reason, it is always a positive factor in building good members in societies. It is very sure that unless speeches are turned into deeds, they will remain harmful.

74. If you do not quarrel, no one on earth will be able to quarrel with you. ... Recompense injury with kindness. ... To those who are good I am good, and to those who are not good I am also good; thus all get to be good. To those who

are sincere I am sincere, and to those who are not sincere I am also sincere; and thus all get to be sincere. ...The softest thing in the world dashes against and overcomes the hardest. ... There is nothing in the world softer or weaker than water, and yet for attacking things that are firm and strong there is nothing that can take precedence of it. The female always overcomes the male by her stillness. (p.656) "Lao-tze"

Reflection: This peacefulness of thoughts can only be seen in the Christ words. Kindness, goodness, forgiveness, sincerity and softness are all strong characters in the man's personality. Each of them is a keystone to start building a very unique individual whose deeds are the dreams of others and whose characters are the magnetism to others.

75. To the Chinese, Lao-tze, the ideal is not the pious devotee but the mature and quiet mind, the man who, though fit to hold high place in the world, retires to simplicity and silence. Silence is the beginning of wisdom. The wise man does not speak, for wisdom can be transmitted never

by words, only by example and experience. He who knows (the way) does not speak about it; he who speaks about it does not know it. He (who knows it) will keep his mouth shut and close the portals of his nostrils. (p.656)

Reflection: None of us can count himself devoted to an ideology unless he is fully soaked and pregnant with this ideology. And this requires a certain depth of knowledge and maturity concerning this exact ideology. The higher one goes to attain a definite place in his society, the more silent he becomes and the abler to listen to others. Because without quietness one can never be capable of encompassing the torrent of the various ideas. This is why he is to be apt to listen more than speak, and to act and to set himself as the needed example. When one reaches this level of wisdom, he leads and he becomes the way which is to be unquestionably followed. This what was the status of Jesus Christ.

76. The wise man is modest, for at fifty-one should have discovered the relativity of knowledge

and the weakness of wisdom; if the wise man knows more than the other men he tries to conceal it;" he will temper his brightness, and bring himself into agreement with the obscurity of the others; he agrees with the simple rather than with learned, and does not suffer from the novice's instinct of contradiction. He attaches no importance to riches or power, he reduces his desires to an almost Buddhist minimum. (p.657)

Reflection: Very simple. The wise man is like the lantern. He must not deal with useless conversation, but he must put himself in the service of the misled ones in order to enlighten them and bring them from the darkness to the light. He links himself wisely to the simple ones to show them the simplicity of the correct way.

77. I am not concerned that I have no place; I am concerned how I may fit myself for one. I am not concerned that I am not known; I seek to be worthy to be known. (p.661)

Reflection: the problem nowadays is that once we have a favorite place for us, we get unwillingly addicted to it. Thus, this place becomes the tenant and we the place. Consequently, this place will be known as the place of somebody, and it becomes more important than we are. For example, can we distinguish the greater importance between the phantom of the opera and the opera of the phantom?

78. Passing through rugged and deserted mountains on their way, they were surprised to find an old woman weeping beside a grave. Confucius sent Tsze-loo to inquire the cause of her grief. "My husband's father," she answered," was killed here by a tiger, and my husband also; and now my son has met the same fate." When Confucius asked why she persisted in living in so dangerous a place, she replied: "There is no oppressive government here." "My children," said Confucius to his students," remember this. Oppressive government is fiercer than a tiger."(p.662)

Reflection: To kill a tiger takes lesser toil than to kill a system which is oppressing the people. So according to Confucius, the danger that a tiger can put on a certain person's life is far lighter than the oppression by a government. The question here is that can one choose a state to live in peacefully? I strongly doubt unless his parents can take this decision.

79. The first principle of good government is good example. (p.663)

    Reflection: If the priority scale of the government is shuffled, whatever the example it tries to set will be mistaken, for it will not be for the right people nor for the right times. It would have lost the chance to set the necessary example.

80. Virtue and beauty so often come in separate package. (p.663)

    Reflection: It is all about the magic of the natural equilibrium. As long as beauty represents the physical aspects and appearance of the individual, and since it always has the first impact, so it may assure the lead in influencing on others or the beholders. Furthermore, the inside of the human being usually takes more time and harder tasks to be uncovered; which in its turn completes the entire understanding and the real reality of the man. Consequently, it is very obvious to be tardy to find the exact essence of what composes the genuineness of the others. Rare are the times when one can be attracted by the inner before the outer components of the man. but the delay to the discovery of the innermost is what makes it more precious and more durable and thus it becomes more valuable. This is the origin of the values and virtues.

81. It is the view of life that we shall take when we round out our first half-century, and for all that we know it may be wiser than the poetry of our youth. If we ourselves are heretics and young, this is the philosophy that we must marry to our own in order that our half-truths may beget some understanding. (p.666)

Reflection: *Life is about completing a certain cycle in all its walks. Once we are fully soaked of one of them and we are getting nearer to making better decisions, it will then be due to the accumulation of all the knowledge spilt during the first half of the cycle. When we reach the acumen of a matter, at that point we will have the power to tell how important was the first part of this cycle.*

82. "The whole end of the speech is to be understood." "When you know a thing, to hold that you know it; and when you do not, to admit the fact – this is knowledge."(p.666)

Reflection: *On one hand, the more knowledge one can have, the more responsible he becomes to speak wisely. And on the other hand, the more ignoramus one stays, the more responsible he will be to keep silent.*

"It is a sign of an educated mind to be able to entertain a thought without accepting it." "Aristotle"

83. Where the solid qualities are in excess of accomplishments, we have rusticity; where the accomplishments are in excess of the solid qualities, we have the manners of a clerk. When the accomplishments and solid qualities are equally blended, we then have the man of complete virtue. (p.669)

Reflection: Any accomplishment should bear in it the very exact spirit of neutrality in order to be useful for everybody and everything. To do this, an accomplishment should be practical. And to have a practical accomplishment, it should be thoroughly engineered and take into consideration any possible failure before carrying it out. Otherwise, it will damage one on the account of another. To end up a meticulous deed, the solid qualities and the accomplishment must, in any way, be equally blended. Then the doer can be qualified a man of virtue.

84. Intelligence is intellect with its feet on the ground. (p.669)

Reflection: Since intelligence is an abstract noun, it can be concretized correctly only if it keeps its peculiar characteristic within the implementations. No idea is considered subtle unless it is fully executed with the least losses. Otherwise it loses its subtlety.

85. Society rests upon the obedience of the children to their parents, and of the wife to her husband; when these go, chaos comes. (p671)

Reflection: Obedience has a very large spectrum of meanings. It can be interpreted to hold a negative or a positive connotation. However, when obedience is mixed or merged with respect it can only generate very distinguished fruits; when it is combined with disrespect or hatred, the only outcome will be the distress or cruelty. Consequently, the society has a very delicate role in choosing the insight of obedience so it will be implanted in the dogmas and in every day's trend. Then, man will be on the safe side of being taken by the chaotic future.

86. **STATE:** Tsze-kung asked about government. The master said, "(The requisites of the government) are three: that there should be <u>sufficiency of food</u>, <u>sufficiency of military equipment</u>, and the <u>confidence of the people in their ruler.</u>" Tsze-kung said, "If it cannot be helped, and one of these must be dispensed with, which of the three should be forgone first?" "The military equipment," said the Master. Tsze-kung asked again, "If it cannot be helped, and one of the remaining two must be dispensed with, which of them should be forgone?" The Master answered, "Part with the food. From of old, death has been the lot of all men; but if the people have no faith in their rulers there is no standing for the state."(p.672)

Reflection: Around 500 years B.C. and around two millennia and five centuries before Abraham Maslow, the Chinese philosopher emphasized on the most important of all prerequisites for the human being to feel satisfied and to be zealous to produce a better life and lead, it is the trust in his leader or ruler. Since then, rare are the sovereigns who show that they are interested in their subjects' survival and satisfaction. Unfortunately, famine and disasters are the pressing forces on the shoulders of the majority of man throughout history. This is due to a mutual fake confidence between rulers and ruled.

87. **Statesmen:** Ke-K'ang asked Confucius about government, saying, and "What do you say to killing the unprincipled for the good of the principled?" Confucius replied, "Sir, in carrying on your government, why should you use killing at all? <u>Let your evinced (revealed) desires be for what is good, and the people will be good.</u> The relation between superiors and inferiors is like that between the wind and the grass. The grass must bend when the wind blows across it. <u>He who exercises government by means of his virtue may be compared to the north polar star, which keeps its place, and all the stars turn towards it</u>. Ke-K'ang asked how to cause the people to reverence their ruler, to be faithful to him, and to urge themselves to virtue. The

Master said, "Let him preside over them with gravity – then they will reverence him. Let him be filial and kind to all – then they will be faithful to him. Let him advance the good and teach the incompetent – then they will eagerly seek to be virtuous."(p.672)

Reflection: *"As you shall be given to you" is a quote from the Hadith of the Islamic creed. However, Confucius is counter saying this quote by asking the rulers to be good, so the people will be good, too. He is asking to practice the act of governing with virtue in order to be followed. A leader who leads by the light of virtue will never take the people to be doomed.*

88. The centralization of wealth is the way to scatter the people, and let it be scattered among them is the way to collect the people. (p.673)

Reflection: *Look at this very effective policy of economical tactic. It is so feasible today if the goal of the state is the sole good of the people, but not the sole good of rulers. A hungry person can easily be misled into wars and can be easily governed and enslaved. Here Confucius is not only talking of the substantial meaning of wealth but also all possible kinds of wealth — spiritual, physical, social or intellectual. And by collecting people, he wants to emphasize on keeping the equilibrium as the lone criterion.*

89. When one has mastered the music completely and regulates his heart and mind accordingly, the natural, correct, gentle and sincere heart is easily developed, and joy attends its development. (p.673)

   Reflection: Each pot filters what includes. When one's heart is filled with joy and bounty, he can never reflect but only joy and bounty. And in order to have one's heart full of joy and bounty, he has to accept and to experience happily these two attributes.

90. Benevolence is akin to music, and righteousness to good manners. (p.673)

Reflection: *These days not all kinds of music are seen as peaceful music. But righteousness can never be but parallel to good manners and benevolence. When the philosopher contemplated his thought, it was correct to an extreme extent.*

91. Let me write the songs of a nation and I care not who makes its laws "Daniel O'Connell". (p.673)

Reflection: *The songs of any culture correctly reflect the emotions and the history of that culture and within these songs the entire sensualities are embedded. Yet, the laws have always been subject to changes and to dispositions and above all to necessities.*

92. Each man has his rights, and each woman her individuality safeguarded. (p.674)

Reflection: *The distinction between rights and individuality is very sharp. Thus, we have to consider each as a special privilege to a very unique and to a very given person. Rights are given by laws, but individuality is freely granted by birth. Wherever you may go, you be subject to a different set of laws, but your individuality is always and anywhere the same.*

93. Morality is a deception practiced upon the simple by the clever; universal love is the delusion of children who do not know the universal enmity that forms the law of life; and a good name is a posthumous ornament which the fools who paid so dearly for it cannot enjoy. (p.679)

   Reflection: If the clever is a deceitful person, then he will certainly use the morality as a mask to deceit the others who are really and are by nature simple. The more mature we become, the less we believe in the universal love. Because we start to uncover the truths of many people who surround us and then we start to discover bit by bit the hostility upon which many laws are built. After we realize all this, we also start to realize how rarely can we enjoy the false realities masking the persons among who we struggle to live.

94. In life the good suffer like the bad, and the wicked seem to enjoy themselves more keenly than the good. (p.679)

Reflection: This is an eternal dilemma unless one introduces in it the Christian belief. It is true that the good and the bad suffer the same, but only because they are both humans. But what counts here is the cause which makes them suffer; and more, the kind of joy each shares and what if the joy is on the account of the sadness of others?

95. The itch to teach is a part of the itch to rule. (p.683)

Reflection: A ruler is a very straight piece of wood used as an instrument to draw correctly straight line with precise measures. Similarly, a teacher sets the children or even the adults to straightness and precision for life. Unless the ruler is straight, it is not a ruler nor can it produce a straight line.

96. In democracy it is necessary to educate all if the government is to succeed, while under monarchy it is only required that the philosopher should bring one man – the king – to wisdom, in order to produce the perfect state. (p.683) "Mencius"

Reflection: It has always been nearly impossible for a teacher to bring all his students to full success, for his focus will be divided among them. But if the teacher is to give only one student a lesson, as a mentor, it is very likely to bring him to full success for he could concentrate on the deficiency and bring it to order. Likewise, a philosopher can lead a ruler to be wise, for his role is to lead and the rest will follow, not vice versa.

97. Nature is not a temple but a workshop; she provides the raw material, but intelligence must do the rest. "Turgeniev" (p.687)

Reflection: Because we make an essential part of the entire nature, it asks us to keep on working and not just contemplating. Nature has been teaching us to work in order to earn our daily bread, and to thrive in order to gain and reach our goals. In nature one should get benefits from all what she provides, but what one has to do is to get use of his strength and intelligence so he can achieve what he looks forward to achieving. This way, man and nature can fulfill the whole task; otherwise, none of them can make it.

98. Words mislead as often as they guide, and the Tao – The way and the essence of nature – can never be phrased in words or formed in thoughts; it can only be felt by the blood. (p.689)

Reflection: Most words have more than one utility, and can be interpreted in more than one meaning; thus, it has the power of a double-edged sword. For this reason and more, it is as easy to mislead as to keep one on to the safe side. Consequently, the direction told by the heart and felt in the blood is more often correct if one has the good intentions to be as good for himself as to others.

99. Disputation is a proof of not seeing clearly. (p.690)

Reflection: Any problem, whether big or small, must be completely displayed and clearly explained in order to cut short the conflicts. If not, more efforts and more time are to be consumed in order to first find clearer insight, then to start building up a certain strategy to find a final solution.

100. Once upon a time I dreamt I was a butterfly, fluttering hither and thither, to all intents and purposes a butterfly. I was conscious only of following my fancies as a butterfly, and was unconscious of my individuality as a man. Suddenly I awoke, and there I lay, myself again. Now I do not know whether I was then a man dreaming that I was a butterfly, or whether I am now a butterfly dreaming that I am a man. (p.692)" Chuang-tze"

Reflection: Darwinism leans on some aspect of this story to a certain extent. The Chinese philosopher depicts here, in his dream, the way a person takes to accomplish his life cycle. In the very beginning, and as an adolescent, a person lives the easy trends of life because he cannot be responsible, even if misery and sadness are marking his early life. later, he is being transformed mostly unwillingly to a different responsible adult. When he comes to realize all what he had passed through in his life, he becomes convinced of what he is. Thus, the evolution of man is very similar to that of other species but with different frequency of physical, moral and mental states.

101. By using a mirror of brass you may see to adjust your cap; by using antiquity as a mirror you may learn to foresee the rise and fall of empires. (p.702) "T'ai Tsung"

Reflection: History tells the future if it is written and read properly. History helps its reader anticipate the coming events; it assists to cast an accurate preview for it holds in it all the seeds by which future is to be generated.

102. The Chinese believe that all poetry must be brief; that a long poem is a contradiction in terms – since poetry, to them, is a moment's ecstasy and dies when dragged out in epic reams (quantity). (p.712)

Reflection: It is very plausible to agree with the Chinese form of poetry, since the lengthy flow of ideas and description may contribute to a sincere loss of focus. It is like the person who cannot argue concisely. Consequently, he may lose the interest of the listeners by making his point of argument over-explained. The core of the Chinese techniques of communication is to be brief and informative. He who is mindful of the precious Chinese characters can distinguish their skill in being experienced listeners; thus, very respectful people.

103. Abstractions multiply with civilization. (p.712)

Reflection: Here, Will Durant is trying to confirm his point of view by showing the readers that the more the people are civilized, the deeper the conceptions are frequent. In the

*T'ang dynasty, some 600 years A.D. the Chinese
civilization was the most advanced in the world.
Concretization was not so demanded among
people, because they had possessed a very
developed trend of thought. They were more
involved in theories rather than actualities.*

104. What was meant by the astonishing demand
that the ordering of states should be based upon
the proper regulation of the family, that the
regulation of the family should be based upon
the regulation of one's self, that the regulation of
one's self depended upon sincerity of thought,
and that sincerity of thought arose from "the
utmost extension of knowledge through the
investigation of things"? (p.732) (reformulated
from Confucius, *"The Great Learning."*)

*Reflection: All is incarnated in the idea where
the whole can sprout out from a "word", from
which all actions can occur and can lead to an
endless chain of reactions. We start then with self
after the decision, with the closest surrounding,
with the family and the larger circle. Finally,
it reaches the state and the nation. Confucius*

had said it with a skeptical tone but with the passing of times, it became more certain after the thorough studies of the words of Jesus in almost all the gospels even in these apocryphal gospels.

105. Nature is nothing else than law. (p.732)

Reflection: Sure it is not. For if it were anything else than law, it might have held within it a certain minute grain of love, but it does not and it cannot. Otherwise, nature will breach its own laws and deteriorate them all. Imagine a volcano eruption which can differentiate an innocent child from a very dangerous criminal!!!! I will not be clearing all humans when they have the smallest hesitancy to do a crime where any child or any innocent man may be victimized, yet any mighty lion will never hesitate to kill a small gazelle with the coldest blood.

106. The highest statesmanship is the application of the laws of morality to the conduct of a state. (p.732)

Reflection: Any rule relies on the ruler. If the ruler is at the nadir of his moralities, then the state will, by all means, be in lack of moralities and seek revolution to re-adjust itself to realize the dream of conduct and discipline.

107. A nation, like an individual, can be too sensible, too factually sane and unbearably right. (p.735)

Reflection: It is true, for the reason that a nation can never think in its collective consciousness. A nation needs to have a cooperative sensibility and sanity to sense the right or the wrong.

108. In nature there is nothing high which is not soon brought low. When the sun has reached its noon, it begins to sink; when the moon is full it begins to wane. To rise to glory is as hard as to build a mountain out of grains of dust; to fall into tragedy is as easy as the rebound of a tense spring. (p.747)

Reflection: This is certainly the normal cycle of life. whatever the reasons of getting high or low they are always inevitable, since it is very natural for the cycle to complete its circle. It may take a while or an eternity and a while, but it is very certain to come to an end where the keystone must take its proper place.

109. There are as many painters as morning stars, but artists are few. (p.747)

Reflection: We all start as fans, if we continue our hard work, we reach the experienced level. Then, after a long and exhausting trip in the experiments, we will certainly be experts in the field we are striving. However, the climax will take shape next to the state of being artists in the very narrow and rigorous field of work we have long been involved in. This is why fans are very numerous, experienced are less numerous, experts are rare and finally artists are very scarce. Moreover, time will be slipping like sand from among our fingers, but we realize the self-esteem, then.

110. Art lies in the conception rather than in the execution. (p.749)

Reflection: Any chez-d'oeuvre owes its beauty to the one who had the idea first; the completion or the execution of this piece of art comes second to the one who possesses the idea. Because the owner of the original idea is the only one who can clearly perceive its entire form and can foresee its exquisiteness.

111. In my young days I praised the master whose pictures I liked; but as my judgment matured I praised myself for liking what the masters had chosen to have me like. (p.753)

Reflection: It is about a very sharp distinction between immaturity and maturity. One will be able to differentiate between the decisions taken in his younger days and those in his older days only if he can replay in his mind and from his correct memory the pros and cons of the choices he had made when he was younger, or in other words, when he was not that much mature.

112. Heaven was not a place but the will of God, or the order of the world. (p.785)

Reflection: Since Confucius times Heaven was considered as the will of God not a place. It has always been the order of the will of God!!

113. No image-maker worships the gods; he knows what stuff they are made of. (Chinese Proverb). (p.787)

Reflection: Since the word "gods" is plural, it does not possess any divinity attribute; thus, it remains in the level of being made and worshiped or adored. For the real God is singular and He is the only maker. He has never or will never be made or substantialized in any lone matter. In this above Chinese proverb, the paganism is illustrated in images or sculptors.

114. To possess ability, and yet ask of those who do not; to know much, and yet inquire of those who know little; to possess, and yet appear not to possess; to be full, and yet appear empty. (p.801)

Reflection: In here, we can deduce the impossibility of having all of the ability, for we have never been able to do everything.

Moreover, never have we been able to gather all the information, for we still in need to know more. Furthermore, none of us can possess all, or can feel complete.

115. Government must take advice where it takes its funds. (p.817)

   Reflection: As the Lebanese proverb says: "he who stretches his hand can never stretch his legs." The indebted is always under a certain obligation towards the debtor. In economics, the debtor is the controller.

116. Confucianism tolerated the popular faiths on the assumption, presumably, that as long as there is poverty there will be gods; the revolution, fondly believing that poverty can be destroyed, had no need of gods. (p.818)

   Reflection: In poor societies, faith plays the role of a soother rather than a savior, for they are almost always helpless societies, and here comes the faith to make them more tolerable to their poverty. Whereas revolutionists often believe that their revolution is the only way to uproot the poverty and to make them wealthier; hence no need for gods to liberate them from oppression and cruelty, because they believe that they have leant on gods and it was useless.

117. He who thinks the old embankments useless and destroys them is sure to suffer from the desolation caused by overflowing water. (p.818)

Reflection: The old schools have always been the grain from which all the innovations start. The needs that the old generations felt were the stimuli for all the new inventions. The best of all advice is the one which is taken from your grandparents. It is a sign of social degradation when we free ourselves from being responsible of our parents and grandparents when they get old.

118. Every chaos is a transition. In the end disorder cures and balances itself with dictatorship; old obstacles are roughly cleared away, and fresh growth is free. Revolution, like death and style, is the removal of rubbish, the surgery of the

superfluous; it comes only when there are many things to die. (p.823)

Reflection: It is like the fire that cleans all the unnecessary shrubs and old broken trees in a forest. The regular fires work as regulators to the ecosystems in a forest even if some species are endangered, for new trees are being able to grow and new spaces are cleared to let the ecosystem regenerate. Likewise, wars and revolutions clear the cruel and the tyrant to make room for new rulers to grow and find again the desirable balance. These new rulers, in their turn, will be cleared away by another revolution or war.

JAPAN

119. The great man has no seed. (p.837)

Reflection: It can be correct for two different reasons. Either the great man becomes great because he has discovered that he is seedless, or his obsession made him prematurely uninterested in giving offspring.

120. The basic principle of Japanese feudal society was that every gentleman is a soldier, and every soldier a gentleman. (p.846)

Reflection: Here lies the sharpest difference between the Chinese and the Japanese insights. In China it is absolutely known that every gentleman is a scholar. As a result, it is a pacifist nation. Whereas in Japan it becomes a warring nation. And history can give many examples.

121. One must learn to see as much beauty in one flower as in a thousand. (p.858)

Reflection: The very same beauty which one can find in a single flower can be found in all the same flowers that resemble it, but the difference lays in the surrounding and the background; moreover, in the purpose and in the way one looks at this flower.

122. A dwelling plainly simple, esthetically perfect, and architecturally unique. (p.859)

Reflection: The necessity led the Japanese to create their own structures of homes. Due to the frequent earthquakes, they knew how to build their homes in a very simple way, perfectly beautiful and uniquely engineered.

123. Seclusion is one method, and is good; but a superior man rejoices when his friends come. A man polishes himself by association with others. If he shuts himself away from everything and everybody, he is guilty of violating the great way. Even if one withdraws himself from human relation, cutting out the relation of master and subject, parent and child, he is not able to cut out love from himself. It is selfishness to seek happiness in the future world. Think not that God is something distant. But seek for him in your own hearts; for the heart is the abode of God. (p.868)

Reflection: *The more a man has contact with people of all walks of life, the more he be refined. When he locks himself up from others, he will be guilty of cowardice, for he proves that he cannot face the problems of life. Thus, the love that he has in him, remains for himself, and his selfishness grows to be very self-centered.*

Consequently, he loses the capability to success in dealing with the outer world.

124. The aim of learning is not merely to widen knowledge but to form character. Its object is to make us true men. The moral teaching which was regarded as the trunk of all learning in the schools of the olden days is hardly studied in our schools today, because of the numerous branches of study required. No longer do men consider it worth to listen to the teachings of the ancient sages of the past. Consequently, the amiable relations between master and servant, superior and inferior, older and younger are sacrificed on the altar of the god called "Individual Right". The chief reason why the teachings of the sages are not more appreciated by the people is because scholars try to show off their learning, rather than to make it their attempt to live up to the teachings of the sages. (p.869)

Reflection: This is why education comes before learning. With knowledge comes responsibility and manhood. Nowadays, the individualism is unfortunately crushing the conformity and as a result, the person is often seeing affairs prior to that of his society. By this, the good teacher is underestimated, while the student overestimates himself when he knows very little according to what he has to see. Unfortunately, teaching is losing its sacred meaning for the student as a consumer or client.

125. Children, you may think an old man's words boring; yet, when your father or your grandfather teaches, do not turn your head away, but listen. Though you may think the tradition of your family stupid, do not break it into pieces, for it is the picture of the wisdom of your fathers. (p.869)

Reflection: It is all about bad bridging between the old school and the new one. The continuity of the old school must be based on the successful communication with its students who make the new generation and further the new school. On the other hand, it is very normal to the new generations to show a certain refusal for their ancestors, for they have not yet acquired the same level of experience as their predecessors.

It is mostly the charge of the parents to find a way to bridge this gap that is often responsible of the deterioration of the societies.

126. Do not let a day slip by without enjoyment. Do not allow yourself to be tormented by the stupidity of others. Remember that from its earliest beginnings the world has never been free from fools. Let us not then distress ourselves, nor lose our pleasure, even though our own children, brothers and relations, happen to be selfish, ignoring our best efforts to make them otherwise. Sake (spirit) is the beautiful gift of Heaven. Drink in small quantities it expends the heart, lifts the downcast spirit, drowns cares, and improves the health. Thus it helps a man and also his friends to enjoy pleasures. But he who drinks too much loses his respectability, becomes over talkative, and utters abusive words like a madman. Enjoy Sake by drinking just enough to give you a slight happiness, and thus enjoy seeing flowers when they are just bursting into bloom. To drink too much and spoil this great gift of Heaven is foolish. (p.870)

Reflection: It is your responsibility to seek joy in each hour you spend, for no one is taking into his accounts whether you are content or not. Nobody will be responsible of your agenda to take the hardship to insert moments of joy in it even the persons you think they are close to you. Seek the causes of joy, even the alcohol, for it is healthy in its moderate quantity for both spirit and health.

127. Those who can enjoy the beauty in the Heaven above and the Earth beneath need not envy the luxury of the rich, for they are richer than the richest. (p.870)

Reflection: Richness is relative. Those who have the capacity to feel the happiness which dwells beyond everything palpable are the happiest of all, because what stimulates their happiness is not consumable, but it lives forever.

128. Of what use was the bravery of a knight against the immoral insignificance of a shell? (p.913)

Reflection: *When a shell falls and explodes, it does not at all distinguish the brave from the coward. It sweeps everybody with full indifference and cruelty.*

EXTRACTED BY WADIH BARAKAT
FOR THE OBJECTIVE OF THE STUDY
ON THE 29TH OF APRIL 2009

CHAPTER 2

THE LIFE OF GREECE. VOL.2

CRETE:

1. It is as difficult to begin a civilization without robbery as it is to maintain it without slaves. (p. 10)

    Reflection: Any civilization, in order to start to take shape, needs a torrent of events. Not taking into consideration whether the occurring events are good or bad, but finally this very civilization will trim itself to sustain all the essential elements to make itself apt to survive. Thus, corruption and misdeeds are important factors to help finalize the ultimate shape of this newly born civilization.

Before Agamemnon:

2. Grandeur is gone; simplicity and consolation remain. Civilizations come and go; they conquer the earth and crumble into dust; but faith survives every desolation. (p.32)

Reflection: History fails to totally rub out what is left from any dying civilization. Its shiny era may fade, but the components of its simplicity mark the clear lines of history. Even if some historians try hard to camouflage the basic realities on which this dying civilization was built on. Because historians may change the written lines while they write, but they can never change the deeds that happened in the past, for no one can "write" in the past in order to change history.

The Heroic Age:

3. The good man is not one that is gentle and forbearing, faithful and sober, industrious and honest; he is simply one who fights bravely and well. A bad man is not one that drinks too much, lies, murders, and betrays; he is one that is cowardly, stupid, or weak. (p.50)

Reflection: He who lives in his lifespan times of war must be gentle and tolerant in order to be outstandingly memorably brave in battles.

He must believe in a certain honest doctrine and must believe in it with a clear head. While the man who indulges himself in cowardice will certainly meet the fate of the feeble and stupid and he will be among those who regret their yesterdays.

4. As social organization advances, paternal authority and family unity decrease, freedom and individualism grow. (p.50)

Reflection: This is what is happening nowadays in the name of being civilized, and the misusage of the concept of freedom. The deteriorated societies are ignoring the importance of the family bonds which are the main factor of keeping the family and its members safer and socially more organized. Individualism can take place within the circle of family playing the role of complementary part without which the circle cannot complete security.

5. Love in the truest sense, as a profound mutual tenderness and solicitude, after marriage rather than before; it is not the spark thrown off by the

contact or nearness of two bodies, but the fruit of long association in the cares and industries of the home. (p.51)

Reflection: *Thus, love is the fruit of many mutual behaviors and concepts throughout the time of communication between two individuals. After marriage the bonds have to be stronger than before, because here come many responsibilities out of nowhere sometimes. Love may hinder death but not awareness.*

6. The individual members of the family change with time, but the family is the lasting unit, surviving perhaps for centuries, and forging in the turbulent crucible of the home the order and character without which all governments is in vain. (p.52)

    Reflection: *A family member must always keep in his mind that he is forming an essential part of this long-lasting unit which he needs to achieve his goals as well as he must be aware that without him this unit will have more hardships without his existence within it. In societies where families are being loose, the social problems are greater and more dangerous.*

7. Precedent dominates law because precedent is custom, and custom is the jealous older brother of law. (p.54)

Reflection: Laws are normally frequently being changed, while customs, guarded by the parents, are more stable than laws and they are the sole origin of laws. Therefore, customs and traditions are considered the older brother if not the father of laws. Consequently, an endless conflict exists between the traditions and laws, and that is very normal.

8. We know that war is ugly, and the *Iliad* is beautiful. Art may make even terror beautiful – and so purify it – by giving it significance and form. (p.56)

Reflection: Due to the positive effect of the art of writing as literature, we can enjoy reading or writing about wars. Still wars, if thought of, are the ugliest thing that can happen to humanities.

As Leo Tolstoy put it in "WAR AND PEACE":
"war is a must but not a game."

Sparta:

9. To be good was to be strong and brave; to die in battle was the highest honor and happiness; to survive defeat was a disgrace that even the soldier's mother could hardly forgive. "Return with your shield or on it" was the Spartan mother's farewell to her soldier son. (p.81)

<u>Reflection:</u> Still the concept of martyrdom in some societies is one of the privileges to a person. Thus, he would be counted as a good, strong and brave, and as a result, his beloved ones will be counted lucky. In our days, one can be good, brave and honored by the means of his humane deeds, by the means of the amount of love and tolerance he can exercise in his life, and also by the amount of sacrifice he can pave his way to bridge a good relation with the others.

10. No amount of teaching will make a bad man good; no training can turn a commoner into an aristocrat: the evils of the world are due not to the greed of the "good" but to their misalliances and their infertility. (p.94)

Reflection: Teaching is like sowing; if you sow in a sterile land you will reap nothing but only regret and ingratitude. Aristocracy is a culture; it can be strengthened only by the means of practice; otherwise, you lose it. To conclude, the more you live the good, the better you lead your life. you should ally yourself with the good and the fertile in order to make more abundant what makes the world a better place.

Athens:

11. Equality is unnatural; and where ability and subtlety are free, inequality must grow until it destroys itself in the indiscriminate poverty of social war; liberty and equality are associates but enemies. The concentration of wealth begins

by being inevitable and ends by being fatal. (p.112)

Reflection: Natural selection has always been ruling over social levels. You will never find equality even in the most refined societies. Discrimination must find its ways to infiltrate within the smallest veins of social entities so that extremities can be distinguished. In order to gather a great fortune, you have to associate yourself with the ideology of inequality and discrimination; then, when you decide to refrain from being unequal, you find yourself doomed to die by your own wealth.

The Great Migration:

12. The longer he pondered the matter, the more obscure it became. (p.131)

Reflection: It is very obvious when a person overthinks a certain matter, it becomes more difficult to take a particular decision. It becomes so, for he, by taking more time, may find more *disadvantages which makes him more reluctant to venture into actions.*

13. A man's vices (or error) are common to him with his epoch, but his virtues (or insights) are his own. (p.137)

   Reflection: Because every man's bad deed is very easy for propagation, particularly in his time, the destructive results become very common, since the road to hell is usually paved with good intentions. In contrast, every man's good deed is not easy to be copied, for, unfortunately, the force of envy is almost always reigning.

14. Things perish into those from which they have been born. (p.138)

   Reflection: It is very logical and natural to witness the deterioration of almost everything from its very same origin and components.

15. Poetry seems natural to a nation's adolescence, when imagination is greater than knowledge, and a strong faith gives personality to the forces

of nature in field, wood, sea, and sky; it is hard for poetry to avoid animism, or for animism to avoid poetry. (p.139)

Reflection: Poetry, in its perfect style, is the sublime style of language. It is always filled with surges of emotions and feelings. It looks like a young man falling in love and feeling so high. In this style of expression, the poet gives life to everything even the death becomes alive.

16. Prose is the voice of knowledge freeing itself from imagination and faith; it is the language of secular, mundane, "prosaic" affairs; it is the emblem of a nation's maturity, and the epitaph of its youth. (p.139)

Reflection: We cannot find any legal document or any constitution written in poetry, for poetry is full of imagination and far from realities. Here, prose takes the right place to acknowledge the needs and the mature decision of realities. Its straightforwardness clears the way to the easier understanding of the logics.

17. The most unfortunate of men is he who has not learned how to bear misfortune. (p.141)

   Reflection: When a disaster falls upon one and his mind cannot understand or assimilate the bad occurrence, this will lead him to a vicious circle where decay will overwhelm him and finally collapse. Whereas, another, who can assimilate and manage to turn the misfortune to fortune, will, undoubtedly, avoid being doomed to decay.

18. Nothing is, everything becomes; no condition persists unaltered, even for the smallest moment; everything is ceasing to be what it was, and is becoming what it will be. (p.145)

   Reflection: Not any existence is stable, it is always in a continuous development from good to bad or bad to good; better to best or worse to worst, etc. We halt this process when we become totally forgotten.

19.   Never ask what things are, but how they became what they are. A study of the second question is the best approach to the first. (p.145)

Reflection: Causality is the supreme question in order to define the origin of everything. The best diagnosis is based on discovering the right causes of the incidence. The more you know the real components which are connected to create the incidence, the closer you are to uncover the solution and then to comprehend the issue.

20.   You cannot step twice into the same river, for other waters are ever flowing on to you. (p.145)

Reflection: Everything is subject to an unstoppable chain of reactions. Time and place are the responsible of this everlasting alteration of the facts of the past, the present and the future, and of here and there.

21.   As the tension of the string creates the harmony of vibrations called music, so the alternation of opposites creates the essence and meaning and harmony of life and change. (p.146)

Reflection: Without the oppositions no equilibrium can be established. Thus, it is very essential to regulate all the hostilities in order to find the amiabilities.

22. From things that differ comes the fairest attunement. (p.146)

Reflection: The more the roots of a tree dig deeper, the more the branches flourish, and the more the tree becomes brighter. This difference between directions is the only way the nature uses to form the finest result which we, the humans, enjoy.

23. Harmony is not an ending of conflict, it is a tension in which neither element definitely wins, but both function indispensably. (p.147)

Reflection: A guitarist, in order to find the finest and the most accurate musical note, has to fine-tune the string by using the essential opposition between the capstan of the guitar and its bridge pins. However, both are crucial.

24.   A married poet is a dead poet. (p.148)

Reflection: Desire is the key to stimulate passion.
Mostly, the poet is in need to have an instigator.
Without a stimulus, a real poet wouldn't be able
to express his emotions properly. When a poet
gets married, he focuses his feelings towards his
wife and loses part of his power of imagination
on his loved ones, wife or children. Thus,
the amount of inspiration will be consumed
elsewhere. Consequently, his production starts
to fade away and finally dies.

25.   The unattainable love is like the sweet apple that
      reddens on the end of the bough, the very end
      of the bough, which the gatherers missed, nay
      missed not, but could not reach so far. (p.155)

Reflection: Some people believe that the more
they wait for a better and purer love, the
more the love they will find is purer. Still the
facts contradict most of this belief. However,
experience teaches us that the delay between
desire and fulfillment is the chief cause which
makes the love greater.

The Greeks in the West:

26. Every man ought so to live as to be worthy of belief without an oath. (p.162)

   Reflection: Usually when one feels that he cannot fulfill his promise, he adds up more oath to his words so that he would be trusted in advance. Thus, one should not promise if he cannot fulfill what he is up to. Like that he would be as weighing as his words.

The Gods of Greece:

27. It is difficult for beauty to be virtuous. (p.184)

   Reflection: It is very rare to find beauty along with virtues. It is extremely difficult to find equilibrium between these two attributes, for they almost always contradict each other. One deals with the substance, while the other with the soul.

The Common Culture of Early Greece:

28. To be in health is the best thing for man; the next best, to be of form and nature beautiful; the third, to enjoy wealth gotten without fraud; and the fourth, to be in youth's bloom among friends. (p.211)

    Reflection: In conclusion, to be healthy, wealthy and wise is the ultimate goal for a man to enjoy his life to the maximum. If one neglects any part of these, he certainly will not be able to enjoy his life to the maximum.

Pericles and the Democratic Experiment:

29. Those who have occasion for a lamp supply it with oil. (p.252)

    Reflection: It is the responsibility of each lucky person to be in full charge of his fortune. When one avoid being responsible, the nature of the things will throw him out of the game immediately. For others are waiting in line to have his fortune and they are endlessly watching like wild dogs.

Work and Wealth in Athens:

30. Bees are kept as providers of honey for a sugarless world. (p.270)

   Reflection: money like bees is kept as providers of necessities when bad times to come. After all, every good thing whether concrete or abstract, can provide with the sense of security if it is well-kept. Imagine an old man turning the pages of his old photo album, you see him smiling or shedding tears of joy.

31. No civilization has found life tolerable without narcotics or stimulants. (p.270)

   Reflection: Everybody's life, even that of civilizations, needs to be either tranquilized during stormy eras or stimulated during over calmed eras in order to find life more tolerable. And here lies the secret of keeping things balanced.

32. No man who is in a hurry is quite civilized. (p.277)

Reflection: For a man to sip and taste the real flavor of anything or any event, he has to do so in a moderate way. Otherwise, he will certainly lose some of the real meanings of it.

33. No one is more severe with slaves than the man who has come up from slavery, and has known only oppression all the days of his life. (p.278)

Reflection: Lest he returns to slavery, a slave, when becomes a free man, he forgets that he was once a slave and treats the remaining slaves more sternly than ever so that he can secure his position as a free man among the freemen.

34. It is true that the state come to his relief in time of great stress. (p.281)

Reflection: It is the absolute truth that the state comes to the help of any citizen when he is in a state of helplessness, oppression or misery. In this case, the state will acquire the obedience, the respect and above all the dominance along with the full right to rule.

35. The goddess of liberty is no friend to the goddess of equality. (p.281)

Reflection: The greedy nature of man hinders his equality with others; thus, it is often impossible to find a free man sustaining an equal status with his peers. If it may to happen, he will unconsciously be enslaved by some fictitious doctrine.

36. Individualism stimulates the able, and degrades the simple; it creates wealth magnificently, and concentrates it dangerously. (p.281)

Reflection: Individualism, in its selfish character, makes the person abler on the account of others. As a result, it becomes so by belittling the others. Effectively, an individualistic person reaches his peak of wealth and health by making others disappear or degrade while he exponentially becomes more dangerous.

37. Cleverness gets all that it can, and mediocrity gets the rest. (p281)

Reflection: Most of the times, the clever person gets a small share of the gain; whereas, the mediocre gets the major rest. Unless the clever one can use his cleverness along with his mediocracy, he will have all of it. In nature, likewise, a lion feeds himself on a fair part of his game, but a scavenger and his pack will definitely consume the rest. Whatever this rest is big or small, they never tired themselves to hunt it.

38. The poor man, face to face with wealth, becomes conscious of his poverty, broods over his unrewarded merits, and dreams of perfect states. (p.281)

Reflection: The real poor man, when he is face to face with a wealth which really needs a brave one to seize, crumbles under the burden of toil and responsibility before he reaches them. He then sits down next to his poverty, cuddles it and feels satisfied of dreaming of being rich. This is how and why poverty rules over and over for long times. And this is why most of the rich stay rich; and most of the poor stay poor.

39. Millionaires shall not be created out of the hunger of the people. (p.285)

Reflection: This very theory has always been and preserved as only a theory. For the fact is totally the opposite. Never has any great wealth been accumulated but out of the hunger and misery of the people. History is still proving this.

The Morals and the Manners of the Athenians:

40. Luxury runs into excess among those to whom wealth is a novelty. (p.293)

Reflection: This is what we call it nowadays "les nouveaux riches" or "les anciens pauvres". They usually don't realize the jeopardy of being in a totally new relaxed financial status. And as a result they are being drifted unconsciously into a rush of spending their new wealth on everything luxurious rather than maintaining and investing their money in a program which helps them preserve their wealth. And bit by bit they will absolutely find themselves poor again; this will be more agonizing than being poor in nature.

41. It has always been the law that the weaker should be subject to the stronger ... no one has ever allowed the cry for justice to hinder his ambition when he had a chance of gaining anything by might. (p.295)

   Reflection: It is an unfair nature law, from the human point of view, to find someone who is ready to help the weak ask for a fair help in order to give him a hand to save himself from the consequence of being oppressed. Yet, the poor has always had the ambition to fulfill a dream within him and become freer than his own yesterday.

42. Our greater delicacy makes it offensive to us to preach what we practice. (p.295)

Reflection: Inside each and every one of us, humans, there is a certain ideological hindrance that makes us feel offended in case we tend to speak out our reality. Two main reasons emerge here: the first is that we believe that not all truths are to be told; the second is that by telling a certain truth, we may uncover a certain mistake in us.

The art of Periclean Greece:

43. Men would find it easier to criticize than to equal. (p.318)

Reflection: To equal is usually much harder than to criticize, for to equal asks more indulgence and sacrifice. But to criticize asks an easier faculty in one's mind and soul. It has always been easier to spot the other's faults than to appreciate their good deeds. It is more in fashion to talk negative than to talk positive. And those who can achieve the level of appreciating before criticizing are usually a very scarce group of people.

The Advancement of Learning:

44. Most diseases reach a crisis in which either the illness or the patient comes to an end. (p.345)

    Reflection: It is the natural law of speciation. On any level or for any organism, if he can adapt to a new surroundings, he will certainly survive. If he fails to adapt, he will certainly perish.

The Conflict of Philosophy and Religion:

45. There is neither love nor hate but only necessity. (p.353)

    Reflection: Necessity has always been the mother of inventions. We love because we need either to love or to be loved so we can fill this void in us. The need to a firm surge of emotional flow pushes us to try hard to find one to share the same sensations or complement our wants whether these wants are love or hatred.

46. Chance is a fiction invented to disguise our ignorance. (p.353)

    Reflection: When I don't know how to make a million dollars, I try the lottery and I become more convinced that it will help me be a millionaire. Because it is cheaper and easier. And I forget that the odds are far less to the point of impossibility where it becomes a mere fiction.

47. Happiness does not come from external goods; a man must become accustomed to finding within himself the sources of his enjoyment. (p.354)

    Reflection: When the causes of happiness are substantial, they live only for a short period because the substance is always subject to fade; thus, it has a very short durability comparing to the real value of happiness. However, when the causes of happiness are originated from the depth of one's soul, it will last for as long as one may live, for it is naturally and normally regenerated.

48. Strength of body is nobility only in beasts of burden; strength of character is nobility in man. (p.354)

Reflection: It is extremely rare to find in only one person the balanced mixture of the strength of body and that of characters. Here the famous saying of "Leo Tolstoy" takes its very exact place: "Russia and summer never mix". One of the two must be subordinate to the other. Then the balance will disappear.

49. A man should feel more shame in doing evil before himself than before all the world. (p.354)

Reflection: the living conscience is the key here to feeling shame as a result of bad deeds whether these deeds are before oneself or before the rest of the world. No one can penalize the person more embarrassingly than himself. Crime and punishment must work simultaneously.

50. Idealism offends the senses, materialism offends the soul; the one explains everything but the world, the other everything but the life. (p.355)

Reflection: The policy of taking any decision is based on either idealism or materialism. The amount of needs decides which to build your decision on. In the case of idealism, one may sacrifice the gain of practicality. But in the case of materialism, one may sacrifice the gain of emotions.

51. The good is not good because the gods approve of it, but that the gods approve of it because it is good. (p.372)

Reflection: Each one of us is almost always free to be good or act well, or to be bad or act badly. As each of us can approve or not of the good or the bad. After all, the good remains good and the bad remains bad, whatever the causes and the effects or however the relative view of each one of us.

The Literature of the Golden Age:

52. In every age some men acquire more wealth than befits a man, and use it to spoil their children. (p.386)

Reflection: *if a man can satisfy himself with his daily bread, everybody can have his daily bread sufficiently. But greed is dominating the minds, and the greedy is dominating the hungry.*

53. Life is a comedy to those who think; a tragedy to those who feel. "Horace Walpole". (p.416)

Reflection: *Thinking has always proved that easiness of life consists of only two things, the data gathering and the art of correctly making decisions. Yet, life has always proved that without emotions and a touch of feelings no art can achieve its utmost level, because a man is not an island, and he is almost always dealing with other persons not always with machines and matter. Thus, the comedy can be defined in Horace Walpole as a mere sarcastic comedy where the person is being ironic and very harmful. In contrast, when a man is able to merge the correct data with the needed touch of humanity, his decision will rather be helpful not a tragic one*

The Zenith of Philosophy:

54. Whatever we do is done through hope of pleasure or fear of pain. (p.504)

   Reflection: Avoiding pain is undoubtedly to result in pleasure. Dodging pain is in itself a pleasurable fact. So whatever we do is through hope of pleasure or fear of pain, but rather the mixture of both.

55. Our knowledge of things is uncertain; all that we know directly is our feelings; wisdom, thus lies in the pursuit not of abstract truth but of pleasurable sensations. (p.504)

   Reflection: A wise man should always end his words with: "as far as I know" because the moment he speaks out his opinion or his knowledge, he is under the fact that his knowledge is not the ultimate wisdom nor the absolute truth. For this reason, one must always put his response in a certain cadre of other possibility which may lead to other probability.

56. The use of philosophy is that it may guide us not away from pleasures, but to the most pleasant choice and use of them. (p.504)

Reflection: Never has any philosopher attained the permanent pleasure, for he surely knows in his inner self that the pleasure he is experiencing is but a passing one. Despite this, his awareness can tell him that it is always a transitory pleasure if used wisely that will lead him to another one.

57. It is not the ascetic who abstains that is pleasure's master, but rather the man who enjoys pleasures without being their slave, and can prudently distinguish between those that endanger him and those that do not. (p.504)

Reflection: Nobody agrees that throughout history there was a single person, wise or naïve, who could master any pleasure. But there are many who could use the pleasure in a controlled way. In a way which can teach him to differentiate the offending pleasure from the safe one.

58.   The most impressive spectacle in life is the sight of a virtuous man steadily pursuing his course in the midst of vicious people. (p.505)

Reflection: It is very difficult to walk in the mud and stay pure, (Thich Nhat Hanh). This is why the lotus flower is very impressive and spectacular. We can also reach back to St. Paul's famous quotation: "Shall we remain in sin, so that grace may increase?" (Romans 6: 1)

59.   We should study nature not in order to explain the world, which is impossible, but that we may learn the wisdom of nature as a guide to life. (p.508)

Reflection: We should always be ready to study not only the nature but the nature of ourselves through the wisdom of God in order to not explain the world which is impossible, but to be able to conceive the reality of ourselves which is very possible and very delightful. This only can happen through the love that the Holy Book recommended us to follow.

60. Slavery is unjust but unimportant; the sage will find it as easy to be happy in bondage as in freedom; only internal freedom counts. (p.508)

Reflection: The internal freedom is undoubtedly the inner peace where we are not in need of any external stimulus to drive us to find it. It has always been dwelling in inner corners of the heart and the depths of the mind. The external freedom is always bound to fading material objects.

61. The gods gave man an easy existence, but man has complicated it by itching for luxuries. (p.508)

Reflection: By simplicity a man can find happiness in his life. Unfortunately, his privations miscalculated the reason why and what to gain. As a result, he was drifted away from simplicity to complicated methods by which he thought he could seek and find substantial luxuries.

62. Intelligence is needed to discriminate between good and harmful pleasures. (p.517)

   Reflection: Indeed intelligence is a major faculty in the man's life. If it is used well, it ends him in a good status; if otherwise, it will certainly lead him into misery.

63. Authority will replace liberty in education, for the intelligence of children is too undeveloped to excuse us for leaving to them the guidance of their own lives. (p.523)

   Reflection: This is why obedience is the key and the safe road to leadership. But regrettably, we are using neither authority nor liberty in a well-balanced means in the so-called the modern means of education.

64. Beauty is unity; it is the co-operation and symmetry of the parts in a whole. (p.533)

   Reflection: In nature, all the colors and shapes harmonize naturally. So every natural panorama is beautiful in a way or another. But when it comes to humans' arrangements, we should study the structure of a part in coordination with the whole in order to come out with a piece of beauty.

65. Virtue is not an act but the habit of doing the right thing. At first it has to be enforced by discipline, since the young cannot judge wisely in these matters; in time that which was the result of compulsion becomes a habit, "a second nature," and almost as pleasant as desire. (p.534)

Reflection: for the virtue to become a habit, it needs a continuous process. A process which is empowered by discipline and obedience. The obedience is to start from the young age so it grows into a good habit with the art of mastery. By this it grows into a built-in character and it produces, as a result, the pleasure for all.

66. The fortunate man is he who combines prosperity with scholarship, research, or contemplation; such a man comes closest to the life of the gods. (p.534)

Reflection: *Within one life span, it is very difficult and rare to find a man who can achieve the prosperity along with learning. This kind of fortune is like the diamond formation which is the production of time, pressure and a very unique set of elements.*

67. As ethics is the science of individual happiness, so politics is the science of collective happiness. (p.534)

Reflection: *Policies are the twin brother of the laws which need tradition and customs, which in turn come out from the fountain of personal happiness to embrace the society as one unit.*

68. Each form of government is good when the ruling power seeks the good of all rather than its own profit; in the contrary case each is bad. (p.534)

Reflection: *When the government and its power is incarnated in one person, this one person is biased to exercise his private power, not the power of the system which sees no personal interest but the interest of the community; then the entire system is enslaved to be working for the account of this ruling person. Thus, almost all of the outcome is being focused to serve only the ruling one or ones. And the result is catastrophic.*

69. Noble character is now seldom found among those of noble birth, most of whom are good for nothing ... Highly gifted families often degenerate into maniacs. (p.535)

Reflection: Spoiled children are almost always the fruits of wealthy families, for money has often been the main cause of undisciplined minds and souls. Unless parents use their money as a good servant, the children will undoubtedly be mastered by money.

70. Equality is just, but only between equals. (p.535)

Reflection: Equality is justice only in case of equal potentials. If justice is to be ruling, it has to find a room among comparable persons. If not, equity will surely be the best choice.

Alexander:

71. Energy is only half of genius; the other half is harness. (p.552)

Reflection: When you make yourself an essential part of what you are doing, then what you are doing becomes an essential part of you. As a result, the energy you put in carrying out the task will be reduced to minimum. By this, you accomplish yourself and you will have a greater self-esteem.

72. Individualism in the end destroys the group, but in the interim it stimulates personality, mental exploration, and artistic creation. (p.554)

Reflection: It is the egoism along with the ignorance of the importance of the teamwork that leads to destroy the efforts, the time and the money used to achieve a certain goal. On the contrary, individualism buttresses the excel of promotion of the self independently.

The Climax of Greek Science:

73. Science and art have nothing to show, strength is incapable of effort, wealth is useless, and eloquence is powerless, where there is no health. (p.638)

    Reflection: An invalid person is the person who needs to be cared for because he cannot afford a certain type of care to others. Thus, he will not be able to use what he has as a fortune, gift or talent unless he is assisted by somebody or something to make what he has more useful and fruitful.

The Surrender of Philosophy:

74. "Every reason has a corresponding reason opposed to it"; the same experience may be delightful or unpleasant according to circumstances or mood; the same object may seem small or large, ugly or beautiful; the practice may be moral or immoral according to where and when we live; the gods are or are not, according to the different nations of mankind;

everything is opinion, nothing is quite true. It is foolish, then, to take sides in disputes, or to seek some other place or mode of living, or to envy the future or the past; all desire is delusion. Even life is an uncertain good, death is not a certain evil; one should have no prejudices against either of them. (p.642)

Reflection: *"One man's meat is another man's poison," is a very delicate proverb in which one can see himself on one side one time, and on the opposite side another time. But still one can define his present according to his present needs and desires. Uncertainty almost always prevails.*

75. Understanding is not only the highest virtue, it is also the highest happiness, for it avails more than any other faculty in us to avoid pain and grief. (p.648)

Reflection: *The more you understand your surroundings, from humans and materials, the easier your life will be. It becomes so, because your degree of maturity will be involved in your decision making. Your decisions will be more accurate and can hit a better target.*

76. Everything natural is easily procured, and only the useless is costly. (p.648)

Reflection: Nothing can the nature give us but only for free; it is always given with the least price as if it is given without hardship. The more we create artificial products, the more expensive they will cost us. Nature gives us freely all what she can afford; however, we procure what we create with more hectic charges.

77. Of all the things that wisdom provides for the happiness of the whole life, by far the most important is the friendship. (p.649)

Reflection: Friendship has always been grasped not given. The hunt for a real friendship is the most priceless as it is the most durable and helpful. A real friend is like solid gold, the more you rub, the shinier it becomes. It is as rare as the black diamond. Blessed is the person who can only have one real friend in his entire life;

he will have two extra shoulders to help carry his burdens.

78. The reason why we have two ears and one mouth is that we may hear more and talk less. (p.651) "Zeno"

    Reflection: Once a sage said: "A wise man speaks because he has something to say; a fool because he has to say something".

79. They agreed that knowledge arises only out of the senses, and placed the final test in such perceptions as compel the assent of the mind by their vividness or their persistence. Experience; however, need not lead to knowledge; for between sensation and reason lies emotion or passion, which may distort experience into error even as it distorts desire into vice. Reason is the supreme achievement of man, a seed from the *logos spermatikos,* or seminal reason, which made and rules the world. (p.652)

    Reflection: This is why and how we became "SAPIENS". We could, as we will always be able to be the first connoisseurs of the result of mixing the reason with the sensation. This is the privilege of men to turn a vice into a virtue or a virtue into a vice.

80. When Zeno beats his slave for stealing, and the slave has a little learning, said, "But it was fated that I should steal," Zeno answered, "And that I should beat you." (p.655)

Reflection: A little learning for a slave led to give the master the full right to beat him. Imagine if the slave were of little more learning; Zeno would not have the chance to be the master or at least a master with less power.

EXTRACTED BY WADIH BARAKAT FOR THE OBJECTIVE OF THE STUDY ON THE 29TH OF APRIL 2009

CHAPTER 3

CAESAR AND CHRIST. VOL.3

Etruscan Prelude
The Birth of the Republic:

1. The victors called the revolution a triumph of the liberty; but now and then liberty, in the slogans of the strong, means freedom from restraint in the exploitation of the weak. (p.17)

   Reflection: Things have always been like that. Victory is a victory; whoever the victor is, he will taste the sweet and sour of freedom. For the reason that any acquired liberty comes on the account of the loser.

The Republic
The Struggle for Democracy
Patricians and Plebs:

2. Contentment is as rare among men as it is natural among animals. (p.22)

Reflection: In our days and by the new means of biotech industry, scientists tend to believe that human happiness is based on different grounds from that of animals, unless you are an animist.

The constitution of the Republic:

3. The discipline of obedience developed the capacity to command. (p.34)

    Reflection: No one can understand the rules if he does not abide by them. The time one obeys the rules, he will have them embedded in his characters, and after that, he will be capable to take the road to be a leader.

4. Rome remained great as long as she had enemies who forced her to unity, vision, and heroism. When she had overcome them all, she flourished for a moment and then began to die. (p.35)

    Reflection: As long as Rome stayed in need to be united, to have vision and to produce heroes, she fought for it and stayed united and strong. By this, she could win war after war until she stood on the top of all other nations. After she had reached her goal, she started to decline because carelessness conquered the souls of her heroes. This is why we can conclude that wars, any kind of wars, are some kinds of obligation in order to reach the top.

Hannibal against Rome
Hannibal:

5. He had disciplined his body to hardship, his appetite to moderation, his tongue to silence, his thought to objectivity. (p.48)

Reflection: This alloy, if it is adopted for a long time with steadiness by someone, he will have a strong penchant to perfection. But perfection is not an adjective to us, human beings. Thus, we are always subject to being biased by preferences for our own account. For this reason, this alloy inevitably leads us to self-deterioration and the deterioration of our surroundings.

Scipio:

6. The gods have not given all their gifts to one man. (p.52)

    Reflection: Gods were at those eras like time nowadays. In our epoch, signs and symbols are given to us by mere scientific results and data. The problem is we are not that quick to read and respond to this secret language. Either because we lack the knowledge to decipher these signs, or because we fall back to the fast development of today's exponential speed of data collection. Because of all of this, we miss the gifts.

Stoic Rome
Industry:

7. The older Romans used temples as their banks, as we use banks as our temples. (p.79)

    Reflection: It is very cynical to see ourselves replacing what fills us with security with what empties us from security. If we don't get into defining the roles of a temple and the roles of a bank, we will not be on the safe side. If not, we will get into troubles with ourselves and with others. Finally, a temple should always be and work as a temple, and a bank as a bank.

The City:

8. Man's vanity yields only to hunger and love. (p.83)

Reflection: Vanity comes from the Latin word "VANITAT" which means foolish pride or the lacking of content. This very attitude can only lead to hunger or poverty in some ways, in other ways to the state of over-estimating oneself which we call it also pomposity.

The Greek conquest
The Transformation of Rome:

9. The citizens no longer listen to good advice, for the belly has no ears. (p.89)

Reflection: As Abraham Maslow illustrates in his famous pyramid that the physically insecure person is not at all ready to move to a higher level, and as a result, he cannot at all be ready to reason the importance of the advice given to him. As well, the very satiated person who had long secured all the physical needs, if he is provided with a piece of advice concerning his substantial needs he won't listen to it for he has no fear at all to be hungry again.

10. Usually the power of women rises with the wealth of a society, for when the stomach is satisfied hunger leaves the field to love. (p.89)

   Reflection: It is used to be the case. Nowadays, it is rarely found like this except in old fashioned societies, for women are winning more respectable places in almost all walks of life, and they are becoming more and more partners in responsibilities. Still we are always longing for love.

11. From the moment that they become your equals they will be your masters. (p.89)

Reflection: "THEY" is very controversial here. If they become my equals due to deep and mutual trust, they can never be my masters; for it won't be their dream. If envy is leading them to be my equals, then they are barking under the wrong tree and can never be my equals.

12. He who steals from a citizen, ends his days in fetters and chains; but he who steals from a community ends them in purple and gold. (p.90)

Reflection: This is exactly what happens when the society is blind or blinded; poor or hungry. Above all, when the community members are cowards, they themselves are stolen. Even their dreams and decisions are taken away from them and they become captives.

13. The principle of democracy is freedom; the principle of war is discipline; each requires the absence of the other. (p.91)

Reflection: It is true. However, freedom without discipline is a very detrimental state. To be a free person in a society you must have an acceptable level of discipline. This is why each era of peace in a country has to be preceded by a long and tiring period of educating the coming generations to respect the laws and abide by them. If this period is to come after a period of war, it is designated to correct the people.

Cato and the Conservative Opposition:

14. Discipline is the mother of character and freedom. (p.103)

    Reflection: Bad discipline engenders bad characters followed by bad usage of freedom.

Literature under the Revolution
De Rerum Natura:

15. Reason cannot be the test of truth, for reason depends upon experience – i.e., sensation. (p.152)

    Reflection: the real truth is extremely relative. It cannot be conceived only by reason or experience. Reason must be assorted with some *emotions in meticulously equilibrated amounts in order to sense it as it pleases the person. This process is rarely adjusted.*

16. Life is given us not in freehold but in loan, and for so long as we can make use of it. When we have exhausted our powers we should leave the table of life as graciously as a grateful guest rising from a feast. (p.152)

Reflection: Life itself is given to us for free, but what comes along it is given as a loan. And we are under the obligation to render this loan to others as a gift in our turn, and so on. We can keep this loan as long as we are good beneficiaries. The time we cannot invest more, we should cede the place to others. We should happily cede the place with full gratitude for the ones who had given us this gift and as happily for those who are inheriting it from us.

17. Virtue lies not in the fears of the gods, nor in the timid shunning of pleasure; it lies in the harmonious operation of senses and faculties guided by reason. (p.152)

Reflection: *If happiness is given to us by God,*
one must not avoid it for it becomes a vice.
But what matters is to use this pleasure in
accordance with our wisdom and intelligence
so we will not hinder the others' happiness.

18. History is a procession of states and civilizations
rising, prospering, decaying, dying; but each in
turn transmits the civilizing heritage of customs,
morals, and arts. (p.153)

Reflection: *This procession is the logical railway*
of the wagon of history. If it is otherwise, a
cultural commotion takes place and the culture
will undoubtedly die prematurely.

19. All things that grow decay: organs, organism,
families, states, races, planets, stars; only the
atoms never die. The forces of creation and
development are balanced by the forces of
destruction in a vast diastole and systole of life
and death. (p.153)

Reflection: *Scientifically talking it is very true.*
But what is astonishing here is that long time

135

ago man always related what he had detected on strong relation between implicit and explicit; physics and metaphysics, and matter and ether. The physicists of today are trying hard to elaborate what simply their ancestors, the old physicists, took it for granted.

Caesar
Civil War:

20. How blind and mad a thing human nature is when passion is aroused! (p.185)

Reflection: *When love turns into passion, blindness comes within. One must thoroughly extricate the seeds of passion from the pots of love; otherwise, this mixture turns our good deeds into bad ones, for the seeds of passion are far stronger than those of love as it is very confusing to keep on providing love with passion so long as it is very harmful.*

Caesar and Cleopatra:

21. Soldiers depend upon money, money upon power, and power upon soldier. (P.189)

Reflection: War, money and power bring us into a vicious circle, where one unconsciously is drifted in a torrent of amour-propre and forgets the main doctrine he is fighting for. War is not an easy game to handle, nor is it as easy as we read in history books. One must not play with war, because the final count of wars has never been tearless.

Brutus:

22. The restoration of order required the limitation of their freedom. (p.195)

Reflection: In times of war, the insight of order shrinks to be unnoticeable and the insight of war reigns almost completely and takes control of all our decisions. When war is over, whether one is a triumphant or a conquered, the time of restoring order is supreme to everything.

In this period, freedoms must step aside leaving the main role to the discipline so it can help restoring the damages caused by war. Moreover, obedience to rules and laws is a key to accomplish the rebuilding of a state.

Augustan Statesmanship
The Road to Monarchy:

23. Honesty is the best policy, but it must be practiced with discrimination. (p.214)

   Reflection: Especially these days, an honest person is taken as stupid. But how can an honest person practice his honesty in discrimination? A major part of honesty must be judged by others who can feel honesty. Here the honest person is trapped between the hammer and the anvil.

The new order:

24. The power of wealth checks the pride and privilege of birth, and the hereditary aristocracy checks the abuses and irresponsibility of wealth. (p.216)

Reflection: A wealthy man has a responsibility of using his wealth for good causes. If he can do so, he is on the safe side; if not, he is under the threat of losing both his wealth and his privilege.

The Augustan Reformation:

25. Moral reform is the most difficult and delicate branch of statesmanship; few rulers have dared to attempt it; most rulers have left it to hypocrites and saints. (p.221)

Reflection: when one doesn't dare to venture into the improvement process, others will certainly run for it. Especially the ones who are not qualified to do the job. They do so because they have an ambition to gain a better place in their community. Any society needs to have a continuous program of reformation; or else, it is doomed to decay. One of the chief characters a ruler has to have is to be daring to take the crucial decision and spent most of his time, efforts and money to reform his society morally and physically.

26. A nation must have a continuity of traditions to be sane, as a man must have memory. (p.222)

Reflection: The history of a nation must have a continual meaning in which all kinds of legacies are kept safe and sound, whether they submit changes or not. Otherwise, the nation will be destined to be forgotten.

27. Laws are vain when hearts are unchanged. (p.224)

Reflection: When laws are not solid in the hearts of citizens, and when the hearts are not feeling stress-free with such laws, not any law can secure the stability or the tranquility of the people. Because laws are effective only if they are conceived by the hearts and souls of the citizens, but not in minds and books only.

The fear of the gods is the youth of wisdom. (p.225)

Reflection: Fear of gods has always been disputable, but fear of God, if well understood, has never been distressful or nerve-racking.

The fear of God in its real sense here is the fear of making mistake, regardless whether it is big or small. The more one feels indifferent about committing mistakes, the farther he is to being wise. It is as simple as it is.

The Golden Age
The Augustan Stimulus:

28. If peace and security are more favorable than war to the production of literature and art, yet war and profound social disturbances turn up the earth about the plants of thought and nourish the seeds that mature in peace. (p.233)

   Reflection: It is so certain that each war or disturbance era is followed by a period of peace and serenity in which the minds and souls of people who have survived war and have the seeds of productivity, will find themselves ready to produce the "positive" outcomes of what stirred them to "compose".

29. A quiet life does not make great ideas or great men; but the compulsion of crisis, the

imperatives of survival, weed out dead things by the roots and quicken the growth of new ideas and ways. (p.233)

Reflection: It is the raging sea that makes the sailor a daring and an experienced one mounted by focus and determination. This very furious sea is the only responsible of forging the characters of inventors, pioneers, leaders, and philosophers. They become so, by deepening their thoughts in the fertile mud of crises and calamities, and they turn them into unforgettable beacons for their nations.

30. Peace after successful war has all the stimulus of a rapid convalescence; men then rejoice at mere being, and sometimes break into songs. (p.233)

Reflection: Recovery after success is almost always a swift process. The successful person will move very quickly and unwillingly from the state of agitation to the state of peace. It is a very normal transition, for it is the normal and safe path to rehabilitate oneself.

Horace:

31. The chief charm of the past is that we know we need not live it again. (p.245)

Reflection: The hope of re-living the most beautiful moments we had experienced is the main stimulus to go through them again and again even if to cross to them another time, we have to endure some misfortune by the way. However, unfortunately, no one can achieve this goal, but we keep on doing that because we feel happy only by the hope of doing it again; not by doing it again.

The Amorous Revolt:

32. It is also useful to surprise your lady in the morning, before she has completed her toilette. (p.255)

Reflection: Real beauty does not need any toilette or any make up. It is beautiful because it is genuinely beautiful. Nothing more or nothing less. This is why the old fashion of beauty is seen and classified totally in a different way from that of today's beauty, especially when we are talking about women. There has been different standards and different criteria.

The Other Side of Monarchy Gaius:

33. Sanity, like government, needs checks and balances; no mortal can be omnipotent and sane. (p.266)

Reflection: Wisdom and potential are like summer and winter; they meet but never mix. Very rarely can a person have wisdom along with might. A person can have wisdom with a little might, or might with a little wisdom. Having both is nearly impossible because in order to test your wisdom you need to do it with power, and in order to test your power you need to test it with wisdom.

Claudius:

34. A woman need not be beautiful to commit adultery. (p.272)

Reflection: Not only a woman but also a man. Adultery is an action done by desire rather than love. Desire is linked to one's brain not to one's mind. One follows his instinct when he commits adultery. If one can follow his mind he may avoid it. What one's eye sees is faster than what one's heart conceives.

Domitian:

35. Only the noblest spirit can bear with equanimity (calmness) the success of their friends. (p.289)

Reflection: Save yourself from envy, avoid being jealous, be not a businessman with your friends, then you can neatly appreciate what they achieve in their lives. Thus, you become more mature and you let them know the real taste of friendship and they become more attached to you.

36. They went under because they were above the law; they became less than men because power had made them gods. (p.293)

Reflection: When you are intoxicated with power, you fantasize yourself of being untouchable and above the law, and by this, you lead the public to depreciate you, for you are subjecting this public to rules and regulation while you are hiding yourself from this responsibility of not being equal to this public. Therefore, you become the product of a lesser human.

The Silver Age
The Dilettantes:

37.   Tradition is the voice of time, and time is the medium of selection. (p.295)

Reflection: If you have the privilege of time, you can willingly make your choice. Equally, when you have this privilege, you feel freer to preserve your habits and your traditions, and you become more aware of the usage of every minute of your day, of your year, and of your life time. You can protect your traditions.

Petronius:

38. If you were born in an attic you can't sleep in a palace. (p.298)

    Reflection: ... *But if you realize that your old attic was as comfortable as a palace, you still have the ability to sleep in a palace; in case, it fits your comfort. But if the palace does not make you comfortable, you better go back to your old attic. We are not explaining this physically but rather emotionally and ethically.*

Seneca:

39. I want my letters to you to be just what my conversation would be if you and I were sitting or walking together. I write this not for the many but for you; each of us is sufficient audience to the other. (p.304)

    Reflection: It sounds here like St. Paul in his second letter to his disciple Timothy.(a must-read)

40. The first lesson of philosophy is that we cannot be wise about everything. (p.304)

   Reflection: *Still the famous proverb works well here by saying:" A little learning is a dangerous thing." When you are aware that your knowledge is incomplete and you accept this reality, you can say then that you got an A+ on your first lesson of philosophy.*

41. Philosophy is the science of wisdom, and wisdom is the art of living. Happiness is the goal, but virtue, not pleasure, is the road. (p.305)

   Reflection: *Literally, philosophy is the art of living wisely. But most philosopher throughout history were swept away by many currents which made them change the goal of their wisdom from the happiness of the society into their own happiness due to many side effects that they had assumed that they had them under their personal control. They did so because they adopted pleasure of virtue as the means to achieve the chief goal.*

42. Pleasure is good, but only when consistent with virtue; it cannot be a wise man's goal; those who make it their end in life are like the dog that snaps at every piece of meat thrown to it, swallows it whole, and then, instead of enjoying it, stands with jaws agape anxiously awaiting more. (p.305)

Reflection: Virtue must frame pleasure. If pleasure is out of this frame, it can pollute the thoughts of a man and he becomes addicted to pleasure and loses focus on virtues.

43. The spirit cannot mature into unity unless it has checked its curiosity and its wanderings. (p.306)

Reflection: The spiritual maturity must always be questioned for there are lots of threats that endanger its progress. In particular, nowadays where we find on every corner new doctrines and parasite-like beliefs which pretend to have the recipe of salvation.

Quintilian:

44. It is impossible to become both educated and a gentleman in one generation. (p.314)

    Reflection: Despite its rarity, it is very possible to be so; in case you are brought up in the vicinity of a parental guide which intend to make out of you an educated gentleman.

45. Write quickly and you will never write well; write well, and you will soon write quickly. (p.315)

    Reflection: This is like two fishermen, one is using the dragging net, in which all kinds of fish are caught, and the other is using a very special bait for a very particular kind of fish. The former will spend times and times to choose the good fish from the bad ones, while the other will have only the catch that he desires or intends to catch. The second will enjoy his well-spent time fishing, but the first will vex himself losing time to select his needs.

Rome and its Art
Architecture:

46. All cultures are eclectic in their youth, as education begins with imitation. (p.355)

   Reflection: Most of education approaches rely on imitations and simulations. A student tries to imitate his teacher, as well as nation try to imitate other successful ones in order to accomplish certain goals.

47. No true work can be done without good faith and clean hands. (p.356)

   Reflection: This is the utmost hope. Everybody agrees that clean hands are becoming very rare nowadays. Still we can find some in every corner of the world and in every field of life. That is why one should not lose faith in doing any job truly.

Epicurean Rome
The People:

48. Much breeding overcame good breeding; the fertile conquered became masters in the sterile master's house. (p.366)

   Reflection: Such a dilemma has been around since the first dawn of history. Most of the times quantity surpasses the quality, because it is in the core of the natural selection that in quantity some good quality will emerge and it becomes the mastering category of man who is destined to be infertile after a certain period, and to be conquered in its turn by the qualitative new quantity.

Roman Law
The Great Jurists:

49. Guilt lay in the intention of the deed, not in the results. (p.392)

   Reflection: It is in the depth of the intention where one must seek the bad aims. But it is a very tough task, because the deeper the guilt is, the harder it becomes to be revealed. And when results are seen, the train will be missed.

The Law of Persons:

50. The word *persona* had signified an actor's mask; later it was applied to the part played by a man in life; finally, it came to mean the man himself – as if to say that we can never know a man, but only the parts he plays; the mask or masks that he wears. (p.394)

Reflection: Living behind masks is a lot easier, this is what the author Charles R. Swindoll says in his book "Dropping Your Guard". Every one of us risks changes when he intends to drop his present mask he is wearing. By dropping each mask, one gets stronger everyday by becoming united to another trustworthy man. Taking into accounts that each and every moment we are passing through attracts you to a new sort of threat. This is why it is very difficult to know the real nucleus of an individual.

51. Law tends to lag (wait) behind moral development, not because law cannot learn, but because experience has shown the wisdom of testing new ways in practice before congealing (hardening) them into law. (p.395)

Reflection: What makes the laws endlessly changeable is that they are always under the obligation to be better for today, because today has never had any resemblance to yesterday; thus, there must be a way to change laws according to the needs of the human kind, and because these needs are constantly and rapidly changing, laws cannot catch up with them; particularly from the beginning of the 21st century.

The Philosopher Kings
Trajan:

52. He who is to command all should be elected by all. (p.409)

Reflection: Otherwise, he is to be either misunderstood or opposed by the rest whether *this rest is a minority or a majority. In our days we can see many of the state commanders have opposition within the ruling body or outside; as a result, his rule will not at all be for the good of the entire community.*

53. One might wield (exercise) nearly absolute power if he never used absolute speech. (p.409)

Reflection: Making promises corners its utterer in undesirable places, especially when he makes void promises to people. Most politicians of today's word follow this trend, and they are becoming artists in using this strategy.

The philosopher as emperor

54. Let it be sufficient that you have in some degree ameliorated mankind, and do not think such improvement a matter of small importance. Who can change the opinion of man? And without a change of sentiments what can you make but reluctant slaves and hypocrites? (p.427)

Reflection: *Changing a man's opinion is not at all as important as perfecting his sentiment. By changing his mind only, you either oppress him or enslave him. But by bettering his sentiments, you are elevating him from a low level of humanity to a higher one where he can wash away some of his stress or grief. When you make so as a ruler, you are automatically gaining trust and being the real friend-ruler.*

Life and Thought in the Second Century
Tacitus:

55.   What makes a people great is not its laws but its men. (p.436)

Reflection: *The being is the core basis of all laws, because it is he who adopts the traditions which he inherits from his ancestors, protects them and improves them. And the traditions are the main womb of all laws.*

Juvenal:

56. The root of the evil is the unscrupulous (dishonest) pursuit of wealth. (p.438)

Reflection: Very rarely can you find a very wealthy man who earns his huge fortune without having his hands polluted by some misdeeds. We erroneously confuse between the pursuit of wealth with the pursuit of happiness, for most of us have believed that money can buy happiness in general.

57. Our forefathers complained, we complain, and our descendants will complain, that morals are corrupt, that wickedness holds sway (power), that men are sinking deeper and deeper into sinfulness, that the condition of mankind is going from bad to worse. (p.439)

Reflection: This is an unbeatable trend of thoughts to all the generations. This exact idea dwells in the minds and is rooted deeper in our minds because we are getting older and older every day. And because of this, we are being farther from our present days' needs and because we are not anymore in command of the changes we are being subjected to. And by being much farther, we become less aware of the necessities the society is seeking. But we can still stick to the ethics which can lead our societies to a safe shore. These ethics, which are also inherited from our grand- grandfathers, and which are also subject to change, are not subject to lead us into corruption, wickedness, or even sins.

58. Around the immoral hub of any society is a spreading wheel of wholesome life, in which the threads of tradition, the moral imperatives of religion, the economic compulsions (pressures) of the family, the instinctive love and care for children, the watchfulness of women and policemen, suffice to keep us publicly decent and moderately sane. (p.439)

Reflection: All these requirements that loom around the entire life of each of us are really hectic if we cannot synchronize among them.

Despite this hard fact, we should strongly believe that these hardships are main reasons to forge us into good members in our societies.

The Cultural Decline

59.   Youth does not come twice to a man, a nation, a literature, or a language. (p.442)

Reflection: It is the life's cycle for every living being. Not only the youth which comes only once, but adulthood, too. However, the span of youth can be prolonged as much as this living being considers it profoundly.

60.   Nothing reaches maturity except through the fulfillment of its own nature. (p.442)

Reflection: Maturity lies its basis on the youth period. The more correct one can lead a young life, the more mature he will be in the next phase of his life. It is a matter of action and reaction, a continuous chain.

Roman Greece
Epictetus:

61. Philosophy does not mean reading books about wisdom, it means training oneself in the practice of wisdom. (p.491)

Reflection: If philosophy keeps itself in theory, it becomes detrimental. But if a philosophy student stops reading and gives himself time to rend his words and ideas to actions, he then steps a move forward into being a real philosopher.

62. Seek not that the things which happen to you should happen as you wish, but wish the things that happen to be as they are, and you will find tranquility. (p.492)

Reflection: No one can control all the happenings and their causes in life. But one should rather try to find a way to adapt to the happenings and then try to change within them. Although it seems very nearly impossible, one can become an expert in doing so with time.

*One must not fear the fire if he wants to become
a brave firefighter.*

63. If a man is reported to have spoken ill of you,
make no defense, but say, he did not know the
rest of faults, else he would not have mentioned
only these. (p.493)

*Reflection: This type of inner defense rises from
the bottom of sanity and knowledge of one's
self. It may hold within it a sort of meanness
and ill-will, or it may hold the real spirit of
understanding and forgiveness.*

The Hellenistic revival
Prose:

64. The wise man will understand that the simple
mind needs simple ideas and pictorial (clear)
symbols. (p.522)

*Reflection: This is why a good teacher can give
a variety of examples to his students. And this
is why the kids can easily understand the ideas
by giving them illustrations on pictures so they*

can assimilate easier what to be understood. And also this is why Jesus taught the disciples by examples first of all. As a result, a teacher, whoever he is, must acquire the ability to let the scholars see the issue from different angles by giving different examples on one question.

The Apostles
Paul The Martyr:

65. Conduct is the test of virtue. (p.592)

Reflection: The behavior of each one of us is the main matrix of our characters. Our comportments can tell very frankly who we are if there is a good reader to them. Whenever we act whatever we act, a hidden part of us is revealed to the beholders, if there are beholders. Finally, our virtues are being constantly examined by our conducts. We can name them the conductor of our characters.

The Growth of the Church
Plotinus:

66. The zest dies down when the speaker feels that his hearers have nothing to learn from him. (p.608)

Reflection: Even the best orator in history will speak nonsense if he is not well and deeply listened. As if you are lighting the way to blind people, or play the best of music to deaf people.

**EXTRACTED BY
WADIH BARAKAT
FOR THE OBJECTIVE
OF THE STUDY**

ON THE 11ᵀᴴ OF August 2010

CHAPTER 4

THE AGE OF FAITH

The progress of Christianity

1. I praise marriage, but because it produces me virgins. (p:53)

   Reflection: St. Jerome here explain why he prefers chastity on marriage. And he shows only one reason why he does so. And he added that he would cut down by the ax of virginity the wood of marriage.

2. Seek not to understand that you may believe, but believe that you may understand. (p:70)

   Reflection: St. Augustine explains how to fortify your faith before you fortify your intelligence by his saying that faith must precede understanding.

3. Even faith is not enough for understanding; there must be a clean heart to let in the rays of the divinity that surrounds us. (p:70)

Reflection: St. Augustine tries to insist on the purity of heart which can ease the path of faith.

Europe takes form

4. Eminence makes enemies. (p:100)

Reflection: Eminence is distinction and importance. When one becomes more important and distinctive, he automatically acquires more enemies who envy him or dream to take his post. This usually takes place when the enviers are not potent to act like the eminent person.

5. In all adversity of fortune, it is the most unhappy kind of misfortune to have been happy. (p:101)

Reflection: The greater the hardship in realizing anything, the greater the happiness that will be engendered after realization. Then, the amount of joy will certainly surpass and remove all the sensations of hardship.

Justinian

6. The lives of all great men remind us all how brief immortality is. (p:103)

   Reflection: The essence of immortality lies only in the perception of the true believers that life ends its earthly chapter on earth, then it begins its next immortal chapter. Whereas the essence of mortality lies only in the perception of the believers that life ends its earthly chapter, and final full stop. In both cases we are reminded of the briefness of immortality. The only exception resides in our capacity of memorizing the person and their deeds after their death.

Byzantine civilization

7. Thrift is a virtue which, like most others, must be practiced with discrimination. (p:120)

   Reflection: To economize is good; to economize too much is too bad. Like any other good characters, being thrifty must be practiced with taste and prudence.

8. If peace comes, historians will have nothing to write about, and that miserable tribe of tragedy-mongers will cease. (p:125)

    Reflection: Rarely can one find a history book written to tell a peaceful era. Most of the history books are written to tell about wars, disasters and crises. This is why, nowadays, and through social media, most influencers use the negativities rather than positivities to influence the maximum number of people. As a result, negative results will result in negative situation and we're caught in a vicious cycle.

9. An historian who strains his pen to prove a thesis may be trusted to distort the truth. (p:125)

    Reflection: A truth has always been a truth, it can never be incomplete, it is always complete because it is a truth. No truth needs to be proven; the problem is not within it; the problem lies in the power to understand it. Any pressure used to prove a truth is subjecting it to be misrepresented to the audiences. It is as simple as that.

The Persians

10. In all civilized societies, clothes made half the man, and slightly more of the woman. (p:137)

Reflection: Because clothes make half of the man and to mention slightly more of the woman, and clothes are very easy changeable, the appearance almost always is used to deceive. Moreover, civilizations come in package with deception. As a result, it is a natural spectacle which we can see in all naturally developed cultures. This may be a built-in cause of destruction for the culture itself.

11. Feminine charms overcame masculine laws. (p:138)

Reflection: Feminine charms may overcome any law if the law keeper subjects himself to the emotions' interventions on the account of rationality and science.

The Koran

12. A religion is, among other things, a mode of moral government. (p:176)

Reflection: All prime religions throughout history inspire governments to write the basis of their rules which are inspired in their turn from traditions that have been either permitted and enforced by the local religion, or prohibited and weakened by the priests of this very local religion. Recent studies show a common stem for all good moral codes among today's religions.

13. Morality is the child of custom and the grandchild of compulsion; it develops co-operation only within aggregates equipped with force. Therefore, all actual morality has been group morality. (p:182)

Reflection: This is what exactly has just been discussed in the previous quote, number12.

But to dig deeper, one has to have a closer look on the causation and the interconnectedness among the cause and the effect of each and every custom and how it became a part of a law from one side; and from another side, the cause and effect of each and every custom and the forces that made this custom ready to become a part of a certain law.

The Sword of Islam

14. The virtues of a saint may be the ruin of a ruler. (p:195)

   Reflection: Very rarely can one see through history that a ruler had taken a saint as his idol. A virtue's way has always been the frustration of that a ruler.

15. Ten dervishes can sleep on one rug, but two kings cannot accommodate in an entire kingdom. (p:197)

   Reflection: It is the humbleness that can make the narrow spaces more comfortable than it is seen. And it is the arrogance that can make the whole planet a very narrow place. This is why it is very rare and very difficult to find two roosters in one coop without being in constant fight.

The Islamic Scene

16.   The willowy (supple) slave girls danced till the men were their slaves. (p:234)

Reflection: The same thing happens when a belly dancer dances in a sensual way to a certain extent where the man watching her starts to disregard the artistic meaning of the dance and goes to the sensual level where he becomes dragged to a state of hollow trance and forgets his dignity and becomes the slave of the wavy body movements of the dancer.

Thought and Art in Eastern Islam

17.   Art is significance rendered with feeling through form; but the feeling must accept discipline, and the form must have structure and meaning, even if the meaning outreach the realm of words. This is the art of illumination, as of the profoundest music. (p:277)

Reflection: Any form of art has meanings only if touches the senses, stirs emotions or awake a certain memory in one's mind. Sometimes, this touch can generate another artistic result, which we call it today the inspiration or the cause of inspiration. This stimulation chain can lead to the sublime art which is called "chez-d'œvre".

18. Wine is as the body, music is as the soul, joy is their offspring. (p:279)

Reflection: Thus, wine is physical, and music is spiritual. Each engenders a different kind of joy. The physical one is temporary and has a certain limit to others, while the spiritual lasts longer and spreads to a larger portion of people.

Western Islam

19. Nothing fails like success. (p:285)

Reflection: When one seeks success with a strong determination, he must accept failure as a part of a successful process. As Winston Churchill *had once put it: "Success is going from failure to failure without losing enthusiasm."*

20. The ardor that destroys is seldom mated with the patience that builds. (P:296)

Reflection: Almost always the love to build is accompanied with the love to destroy. If you want to build a house, you are obliged to destroy a natural habitat of certain species. However, while you are preparing the land for construction, and by this you are demolishing some natural habitat form some species, you still feel a certain kind of joy because you are building your house. And this principle is practiced on many other fields.

21. The poor welcomed him, always preferring new masters to old. (P:307)

Reflection: Because the poor always have high hopes in a new ruler, forgetting the history lessons that there has never been a new invader better than an old tyrant. The devil that we know is better than the one who we don't know. The older the ruler is on his throne, the milder he becomes, because he becomes more acquainted and to the way the poor live.

Grandeur and decline of Islam

22. Nothing, save bread, is so precious to mankind as its religious beliefs; for man lives not by bread alone, but also by the faith that lets him hope. (P:343)

Reflection: As in the gospel of Matthew 4:4, the hope in the salvation due the belief in the word of God. The pricelessness of the hope is unquestionable in the walks of life of every man. Without hope to one's will and without bread to one's body, no man will be able to fight for a better tomorrow.

The Talmud

23. Descend a step in choosing a wife; ascend a step in choosing a friend. To marry a woman above one's rank is to invite contumely. (p:362)

Reflection: In fact it is not at all a matter of stepping up or down in choosing either a wife or a friend, for both choices, like any choice you take, can either harm you or endorse you. it is a matter of the choice itself and its advantages to you a chooser.

The Decline of the West

24. Beliefs make history, especially when they are wrong; it is for errors that men have most died. (p:458)

Reflection: Indeed it is for errors that men died and still dying. The most outstandingly death throughout history, all history, is that of Jesus Christ. He died because of our errors, and because our wrong beliefs. Nevertheless, history is still writing on Him throughout our right beliefs in His words.

25. One man, one lifetime, had not availed to establish a new civilization. (p:472)

Reflection: To produce a doctrine, a culture or a nation an era of many lifetimes is needed. No one can witness the rise and fall of a civilization. One can witness some turning points or corners in the course of an existing civilization.

26. God does not know evil, for if He knew it, He would be the cause of it. "Johannes Scotus Eriugena / Erigena" (p:477)

Reflection: The will is free in both God and man. This is what Eriugena had concluded in his treatise "De Divina Praedestinatione". However, as human beings, we cannot always defend in practice the doctrine of the absolute free will, for we run or hide preferring to discharge ourselves from the responsibility of a mistake and put it on the fate, the chance, coincidence, or God sometimes. All of this prove our weakness not the absence of the free will.

27. Authority sometimes proceeds from reason, but reason never from authority. For all authority that is not approved by true reason seems weak. But true reason, since it rests on its

own strength, needs no reinforcement by any authority. (p:477)

Reflection: Reasoning is calculation and explanation. Thus, reason doesn't need any authority. Any principle that is not based on reason will not survive and always will be a controversial one, as it cannot exercise any authority. The reason has always been the basis of power.

28. We should not allege the opinions of the holy fathers... unless it is necessary thereby to strengthen arguments in the eyes of men who, unskillful in reasoning, yield rather to authority than to reason. Here is the Age of Reason is moving in the womb of the Age of Faith. (p:477)

Reflection: Unfortunately, nowadays, we seek reason in order to believe. We confuse ourselves by equaling the verb to believe and the verb to trust. To believe is to love, to want and to like without the need to a scientific reason, while to trust is to acknowledge the truth of a thing. This is why the short-sighted man always needs a certain explication or examples in order to be promoted from trust something or someone to believing in that something or someone.

The Rise of the North

29. Men wear out rapidly in war or government. (p:492)

   Reflection: A man who is submitted to an overcharge of responsibility in wars or government brings to himself instability of body and soul. The instability of body is seen on his outside appearance, but the most dangerous is the psychological instability which inflicts dangerous wounds upon his behavior and decisions.

30. History seldom destroys that which does not deserve to die; and the burning of the tares makes for the next sowing a richer soil. (p:510)

   Reflection: Who does not deserve to die, does not die; regardless to the causes and effects. Meanwhile, he surely has another mission to complete; in such a way, history can write another chapter. Those who die will fill the blank lines in history books. Others turn will come sooner or later.

Christianity in Conflict

31. It is reserved to the philosopher, and forbidden to the man of action, to see elements of justice in the position of his enemy. (p:551)

    Reflection: A man can be both a philosopher and a man of action. Both states go parallel, they can never mix or crisscross. When a man is in a physical action, he hardly can be practicing philosophy, for philosophy requires a physical stability and stillness. For this reason, a philosopher, in his stillness state, can focus to find some positive elements in his elements and act accordingly.

Feudalism and Chivalry

32. Under every system of economy men who can manage men manage men who can only manage things. (p:560)

Reflection: Who manages who? The person who only manages things is managed by man who only manages man. This does not confirm that the first is less or more important than later. Both are equally and mutually indispensable.

33. It would of course be absurd to expect soldiers to be saints; good killing requires its own unique virtues. (p:575)

Reflection: Sanctity is very questionable. In our new social entities, there is no such a good killing, for killing opposes the insight of purity, and a saint has to be as pure as it needs. Still we can find some war heroes who fought and killed for the ultimate purposes which they had considered righteous; yet, they have been sanctified. This contrast is setting enormous questions upon the suitability of their holiness.

34. Love teaches everyone to abound in good manners. (p:577)

Reflection: Because love can hinder death as Tolstoy had said, why can't love flourish *in good manners. It is very natural to obtain wine from grapes, and good wine from good grapes and skill. The time when we can practice unconditional love, we can achieve the abundance of goodness.*

The Crusades

35. Men must kill with a good conscience if they are to fight successful wars. (p:593)

Reflection: It is as rare as a black diamond or more to kill with a good conscience. Killing and good conscience never come in one package. Successful wars, in all histories, were waged not in good consciences but by the means of brain wash or the blind believes.

The Early Inquisition

36. Intolerance is the natural concomitant of strong faith; tolerance grows only when faith loses certainty; certainty is murderous. (p:784)

Reflection: When one is certain or believes that he is certain of something, skepticism of this thing by others brings to clash. The way to the full belief is always mixed with tolerance and patience, for without patience one cannot tolerate the opposites. This is why the strong belief in something if not seasoned with tolerance it will surely be related to intolerance.

Morals and manners

37. Christianity taught men that patriotism unchecked by a higher loyalty is a tool of mass greed and crime. (p:844)

Reflection: Like that Christianity is becoming universal. Without loyalty and similar characters, without pardon and constructive virtues, there won't be belief in not only patriotism but also in all kinds of doctrines.

The Resurrection of the Arts

38. Those who cater to human vanity seldom starve. (p:849)

Reflection: It is because of the poverty of the majority; the minority can provide sustenance to the poor. It is because of the abundance of wealth with the wealthy; there is always deficiency with the poor. The rich people make their great fortunes on the account of the small fortunes of the poor. This is what the eco-sociologists name it the distribution of the wealth.

The Gothic Flowering

39.   History is a duel between art and time. (p:880)

Reflection: Like the ticking of a clock never ceases, the flow of time also does. Time can never be stopped on all levels. However, art builds its legacy very slowly. Art has always been impacting on humans very softly but very long-lasting. Time slips like sands among fingers; art has its endless impression on cultures and civilizations.

Transmission of Knowledge

40. He who should know the history of words would know all history. (p:906)

    Reflection: The progress and development of languages illustrates the real history of civilizations. The one who can decipher the right track of any language's progress and propagation can understand the real lane take by any culture till its current state. For the reason that in the words of each language dwells the energy which pushes it to survive; thus pushes the culture using this language to last.

The Adventure of Reason

41. God is not a philosophical conclusion but a living presence; it is better to feel Him than to define Him. (p: 959)

    Reflection: Since the good is higher than the true, and the simple virtue surpasses all sciences, it is easier to feel than to define. In

Matthew 5:8 it is written:" Blessed are the pure in heart, for they shall witness God ".

42. The highest knowledge we can have of God in this life, is to know that He is above all that we can think concerning Him. (p:969)

   Reflection: As mentioned in the previous quote, it is not as easy as we think to define God, for He is beyond our scientific recognition. Our scientific knowledge, though advanced, as we think, is extremely limited according to His being. This is why Thomas Aquinas is insisting on the doctrine that God, not man, is the center and theme of everything.

43. Society and the state exist for the individual, not he for them. (p:975)

   Reflection: Sovereignty is from God vested in man. Authority given from God is not like authority given from man. We almost always confuse them. The former needs more love and sacrifice, but the second needs more reason and science.

Christian Science

44. Only a burn really convinces us that fire burns. (p:1009)

Reflection: As the famous Lebanese proverbs put it with a literal translation:

- *"the ember burns where it falls only."*
- *"the only one who can correctly count the whips is the beaten."*

The Age of Romance

45. It is hard to romanticize desire fulfilled, and where there are no impediments (weaknesses) there is no poetry. (p:1037)

Reflection: Definitely, it is very hard and scarce to keep the level of desire and want after the accomplishment of the mission. If morality does not exist in the deep decision mechanism, one cannot preserve the enthusiasm and excitement after the ecstasy of the achievement. Only the factor of love, when it overwhelms the substantial desire, can preserve the sublime feeling and change it to a state of giving and sacrifice.

46. Inquiry is fatal to certainty. (p:1045)

Reflection: Nothing seems certain but only in a given time and place. This is why the quest is a must to keep the certain and to make the uncertain certain.

Dante

47. Partly a great man is great because those less than he have paved his way, have molded the mood of the time to his genius, have fashioned an instrument for his hands, and have given him a task already half-done. (p:1058)

Reflection: Normally an achieved task is achieved due to a well-programmed and coherent team work. But the result holds the name of one person. Usually the leader or the strongest member of the team or even the producer-the payer. A good and honest historian must include in his writings each group member and his contribution in the task. Throughout history, many great deeds or inventions are cited only for the sake of one person and on the account of the rest. If we dig deep, many contributors had more important roles than the bearer of the event name. That is why no history is complete or completely honest.

48. The usurpation (confiscation) of the right does not create a right. (p: 1063)

    Reflection: Jean De La Fontaine says in one his famous fables "The Wolf and the Lamb" that might makes right. Though it is sometimes universal, still it is not humane at all.

    Extracted for the purpose of study By Wadih Barakat On the 12/12/2011

CHAPTER 5

THE STORY OF CIVILIZATION. V

(WILL DURANT)

The Renaissance
BOOK ONE: PRELUDE

Chapter One
The Age of Petrarch and Boccaccio.

The Poet Laureate:

1. There is no lighter burden, nor more agreeable, than a pen. Other pleasures fail us, or wound us while they charm; but the pen we take up rejoicing, and lay down with satisfaction; for it has the power to advantage not only its lord and master but many others as well. (p.13)

    Reflection: The pen incarnates the idea. The invention of writing is still the backbone of all inventions. From the poet point of view, it is only the pen that can discharge him from all the burdens of ideas in his mind, for he takes them as a responsibility do spread to people, regardless to their level of interest.

    A pen is the speaking silence that never betrays its holder. It glows in the midst of the battle of ideas like a sword.

2. Great must be the powers of both body and mind that may suffice both to literary activity and to a wife. (p.14)

Reflection: Indeed, it must be great. One must have a multi-threaded mind to be able not to confuse between the two kinds of powers that he must exercise. Because each kind has a peculiar flavor, and they are always contradictory. The efforts used in literary activity are rarely limited by boundaries, but the efforts used in dealing with one's wife are restricted to unimaginable limits. The consequences of the later are very dangerous.

3. Philosophy aims only to hair-splitting, subtle distinctions, and quibbles of words. Such a discipline could make clever debaters, but hardly wise men. (p.14)

Reflection: Philosophers are always under the jeopardy of being derailed off the right track. They are asked to keep their heads on, too stay focused on their aim and to use the most correct term in order to be able to deliver the right message. Otherwise, they lose the wisdom to become cunning orators or sly persuaders.

4.   How a ceremony could make a pundit out of a fool! (p.14)

Reflection: *Gustave Le Bon once implied in one of his studies (The Crowd), that the crowd never thinks. If the crowd can think, we could have saved the world from lots of many mentally disordered rulers, we could have avoided failing many peoples. However, unfortunately, we, as crowd, we cannot think; though we have a kind of collective conscience, it does not lead us to possess a collective analytical ideology.*

Rienzo's Revolution:

5.   Power, like freedom, is a test that only a sober intelligence can meet. (p.18)

Reflection: *Even the freedom has power. It has power if it is used with lucidity and cleverness. Without lucidity and cleverness, the freedom becomes tyranny and it loses it attractive power to become a repulsive one. Power is like wine. When it is used with moderation, it gives you the*

feeling of governance; otherwise, it makes you
fantasize the governance.

Milan:

6. The triumph of desire over man, of chastity
   over desire, of death over chastity, of fame over
   death, of time over fame, of eternity over time.
   (p.38)

   Reflection: This confusing and logical chain
   depicted by Petrarch during his eight years of
   subjection, explains how well we are bound to
   our weaknesses, clarifies our final destinations
   whatever we pretend we are mighty, and gives
   hope, in the same time, for a better understanding
   of our deep reality.

Twilight of the "Trecento":

7. Eloquence without guns finds no ears among
   diplomats. (p.42)

   Reflection: Adding power to power is a
   successful strategy. When you can convince

somebody by the power of persuading, and show him that you have the gun and you have your finger on the trigger and the might to pull it, then, the persuasion is fully granted. This might not please many of the people; however, this tactic is still dominating the way we write history.

BOOK TWO:
THE FLORENTINE RENAISSANCE
Chapter Four: The Golden Age.

Literature: The Age of Politian

8. The mature mind finds its fullest functioning and satisfaction in the service of the state and the commerce of the world. (p.120)

Reflection: This is the mature mind. Nevertheless, in our days, we find immature minds functioning with self-satisfaction in the

*bad service of the state and in the manipulation
of the commerce of the world.*

Botticelli:

9. Every artist must be a sensualist before he can
    paint ideally; he must know and love the body as
    the ultimate source and standard of the esthetic
    sense. (p.137)

    *Reflection: Real artists have to sensualize and
    imagine the final chez-d'œvre or work of art
    they are on in order to know the way they are
    going to pass to achieve it as they wish. They
    must feel and know the components of their
    work. They must feel it in an awe, and know it
    with science.*

Chapter Five: Savonarola and the Republic.

The Prophet:

10. A faithful dog does not leave off its master's defense because a bone is thrown to him. (p147)

   Reflection: This is the solid core of loyalty. *Physical temptations are to discard your own belief, to weaken your point of strength and to let drop your gun in the faith of what threatens your enlightened existence.*

The Statesman:

11. Complete democracy was postponed as impractical in a society still largely illiterate and subject to waves of passion. (p.149)

   Reflection: Illiteracy is being almost totally eradicated, and we still find peoples are being subjected to waves, large and detrimental waves, of not only passion, but also addiction to being cunningly manipulated by thousands of means of distractions. As a result, illiteracy is not anymore a cause to hinder practicing democracy.

12. Human nature remained. Men are not naturally virtuous, and social order maintains itself precariously amid the open or secret conflict of egos, families, classes, races, and creeds. (p.151)

Reflection: This is the human nature to maintain survival by the means of conflicts. Virtuousness only exist in the morals and in the behaviors of wise. Moreover, the minority are capable to reach wisdom. This makes the majority unwise and; consequently, men are not by nature virtuous.

Art under the Revolution:

13. Skilled in floating on a flood. (p.163)

Reflection: Many potent men have the ability to get use out of turmoil, they have the power to dodge dangers; they can persuade some people that they are either innocent or heroes, as it fits them. Where to many, floods are not rideable, these potent men can do it easily and happily. They consider it as a golden chance to hunt.

14. He who instructs ability and promotes well-being is as truly a father as the one who begets. (p.165)

Reflection: Gratitude to its extreme extent does exist in this quote. Gratitude to the person who is not of your own bloodline and is still willing to give freely his efforts, time money to you as his student. Gratitude to the one who defends you when you are weak to show you how defend yourself when he is not around. Such persons are sometimes more important in one's life than the real fathers.

BOOK THREE:
ITALIAN PAGEANT
Chapter Seven: Leonardo Da Vinci.

In Milan:

15. An artist's most important work lies in conception rather than in execution, and men of genius do most when they work least. (p.204)

   Reflection: Conception is the Big Bang of any idea. The moment the conception is really completed; the rest of work can be programmed. The conception cannot be planed, it can be matured or ripen by reconsidering it again and again. Here lies the most delicate part of the work.

Florence:

16. Poor impassioned lovers! A nature blindly commanding continuance burns your nerves with an absurd hunger for our flesh, softens your brains with a quite unreasonable idealization

of our charms, lifts you to lyrics that subside with consummation and all that you may be precipitated into parentage! Could anything be more ridiculous? But we too are snared; we women pay a heavier price than you for your infatuation. And yet sweet fools, it is pleasant to be desired, and life is redeemed when we are loved. (p.212)

Reflection: When Da Vinci painted the Mona Lisa, some critics believed that the message beyond the portrait of the Mona Lisa is the unfulfilled desire of men to women and of women to men.

The Man:

17. If you are alone, you are all your own; with a companion you are half yourself; so you squander yourself according to the indiscretion of your company. (P.216)

Reflection: This is what I call it the most precious value of the loneliness. Though loneliness sometimes is an evil state for soul and mind, and despite the fact that loneliness is the mother of viciousness, it has still been able to be tamed. Loneliness has its silver lining. When you are alone, you avoid being under the negative effect of the presence of others. Finally, loneliness needs training to dominate it, and it is hard.

18. The Nile has discharged more water into the sea than is at present contained in all the waters of the earth; consequently, all the sea and the rivers have passed through the mouth of the Nile an infinite number of times. (p.216)

Reflection: Da Vinci wanted to explain to us that no given amount of contemplation could tell that it is enough for the achievement of a work. He insists that the more we contemplate, the more we need contemplation. Whereas the intended work does not need that much. Too much contemplation is like procrastination, it steals time.

19. Art lies in conserving and designing, not in the actual execution; this was labor for lesser minds. (p.216)

Reflection: This art master, Da Vinci, asks us to keep on reconsidering our work, for he wants us to come out with the optimal possible result. As a result to the optimal outcome, we will acquire a more developed mind.

The Scientist:

20. Any man's experience can be no more than a microscopic fragment of reality. (p.221)

Reflection: Da Vinci, as a scientist, sees only the sum of skills of all men throughout the entire history can make the real or sublime reality. He was a man of experience rather than experiment. He favored the practice not the test.

In France:

21. As a day well spent makes it sweet to sleep, so a life well used make it sweet to die. (p.227)

Reflection: Before he died on May 2, 1519, Da Vinci wrote the above reflection. As if he was, in his will, trying to advise us to spend our days in wellness so we end them well. Following the famous proverb: "all is well that ends well."

Chapter Nine: Mantua

Andrea Mantegna:

22. Those who desire immortality must pay for it with their lives. (p.255)

Reflection: Immortality to the flesh is like air to the fish. Immortality for human beings can only be achieved by a great amount of sacrifice. A sacrifice of the flesh that is mixed with the unconditional love of giving. When one is

willing to give of his self so that the other will
rise from the dust and torture, then the giver
will purify himself and will be putting his name
on the immortal and golden pages of history.

Chapter Ten: Ferrara.

Ariosto:

23. No man is a hero to his debtor. (p.274)

Reflection: Normally the debtor is the controller.
As the famous French saying tells us:" qui donne
ordonne". Unless the debtor is not a real debtor
but a giver and a helper, he will see an act of
heroism in the success of the others.

24. Why is it that learning and infidelity go hand in
     hand? (p.277)

Reflection: It is said that the teaching is the
most ungrateful profession or mission. That
is not in my case, personally. Teaching is an
inspiring mission. In it, the teacher's goal is to

make his student better than him. Then, it comes the turn of a student to show a certain gratitude to his teacher in case the teacher was a real teacher with a humble mind and character. If the teacher did not feel that gratitude, and it is not a must, he has to suffice himself with the success of his scholars and forget this feeling of infidelity.

Chapter Eleven:
Venice and her realm.

Titian: The Formative Years:

25. He who drinks and does not drink again does not know what drinking is. (p.309)

Reflection: This is a famous and an effective method of learning. Repetition teaches a lot because it holds the essence of practice. The time you do the task twice or thrice, you know how to make it better and how to evaluate and estimate correctly.

Bembo:

26. Fame too, like beauty, can intoxicate. (p.318)

   Reflection: One becomes famous when his deeds usually attract the attention of many people and are generally evaluated positively. In such case, this person is overwhelmed by a pleasurable stimulation of the feeling that he is famous or important to others. The same thing when a beautiful person realizes the attraction of his beauty, his self-realization can be poisoned to the point of damage. Equilibrium is needed as always.

Chapter Twelve:
Emilia and the Marches.

Urbino and Catiglione:

27. The first requisite of a gentleman must be gentle birth. (p.347)

Reflection: It is very necessary for any character in order to be rooted in the personality to be innate. Because it is very normal to have a stronger quality if it is inherited and accompanied by a suitable ambiance to flourish in. Especially when we are talking about gentleness or delicate charms like it.

28. It would be very difficult for one to acquire good manners, and an easy grace of body and mind, except by being reared among persons already possessing these qualities. (p.347)

Reflection: As I mentioned in the previous reflection that the ambiance in which the person is being brought up is, if not the most important, one of the most important factors by which the reared person is affected. It is very easy for the good manners to be ruined by the atmosphere it lives in, because as it is said that the road to hell is paved with good intentions.

29. No court, how great so ever it be, can have any sightlines or brightness in it, or mirth, without women; nor any courtier can gracious, pleasant

or hardie (brave) nor at any time undertake at any gallant enterprise of chivalry, unless he be stirred with the conversation and love of women. (p.347)

Reflection: Castiglione, here, means by court an elite or a high-class society gathering. He wants to emphasize on the delicacy, which the presence of a woman can add to a gathering, for at that time, a woman was considered totally different from our time. Anyway, I agree with him that there must always be the air of a woman somewhere to achieve an optimal pleasure or satisfaction. Following the famous French saying," cherchez la femme, pardieu!"

BOOK FOUR:
THE ROMAN RENAISSANCE
Chapter Fifteen:
The Renaissance Captures Rome.

The capital of the world:

30. Democracy is a luxury of disseminated intelligence, security and peace. (p.375)

> *Reflection: Some say that democracy is a goal, while others a means. In both cases, democracy is relatively appreciated. It has always been, since the times of Romans, a controversial issue.*
>
> *Democracy in its core is to reflect the peoples' understanding and readiness to implement the necessary progress by which a nation can achieve the state of total happiness and ease. In all cases, democracy can only be partially implemented. It can be giving the sense of ease even under dictatorship, socialism, capitalism or even kingdoms.*

Paul the Second:

31. The lives of great men oft remind us that a man's character can be formed after his demise. If a ruler coddles the chroniclers about him, they may lift him to posthumous sanctity; if he offends them, they may broil his corps on a spit of venom or roast him to darkest infamy in a pot of ink. (p.319)

Reflection: In a way or another, historians can be freely depicting and describing the life and characters of an important person after his death. They can do so for two main reasons. The first is that they are not anymore under the obligations to tell precisely what must be told, for he cannot personally refuse any explanation of his. The second is that the school of thought they abide by usually guides them. However, in both cases, historians can falsify the truth according to what they are biased to and according to their own interests or the interests of the ideology they adopt. Unfortunately, the truth has never been entirely known.

32. It is an unwritten law of economics that the price of a product depends on the gullibility of the purchaser; but the poor grumbled forgivably at the thought that their hunger fed the luxuries of the Riarios (riches). (p.397)

Reflection: It is almost always the naivety of the poor or the ignorant consumer that defines the price of a product. You can add to these two factors the strong indispensability that this consumer feels for the purchased product. Nowadays, it is becoming a strategy for the mega producers to make this indispensability stronger.

Chapter Sixteen: The Borgias

Alexander the Sixth:

33. To rulers, religion like almost everything else, is a tool of power. (p.410)

Reflection: To the mighty ruler everything can be used as a tool of power. What if the tool is a very strong one?! Anyway, the rule, as a means of governing, has always been a conflictual issue between the religious and the ruling men. Through history, many wars were waged for this reason and the innocent believers were always the victims; neither the statesmen nor the clergymen.

Caesar Borgia:

34. It is proper to snare those who are proving themselves past masters in the art of snaring others. (p.424)

Reflection: It is almost always correct to wish to others whatever you wish to yourself. At all times, the religions insist on this principle. History always writes about deceivers who finally are deceived by others, as if history is repeating itself.

Chapter Eighteen: Leo Ten

Raphael and Leo Ten:

35. One does not need solitude to be himself. (p.503)

   Reflection: Still solitude helps the person focus on himself, but with a little practice, a person can dodge all forms of distractions and achieve his optimal objective when he is in the midst of a commotion. However, solitude in its proper sense and usage may cause dangerous effects as it help get rid from the negative effects from the cacophonies of crowds.

36. The repetitious contentions of parties and states for power and privilege are the monotonous forth of history, and that nothing matters but devotion to goodness, beauty, and truth. (p.504)

   Reflection: The repetitive and continuous cycle of frequented events sketches the main line of history and the chief trajectory of coming events. As states and statesmen come and go, history engraves both the good and the bad deeds of each of them on its golden book. Moreover, the more this history of events is read, the more memorable they become along with the lessons we take from them.

BOOK FIVE: DEBACLE
Chapter Nineteen:
The Intellectual Revolt

The Occult:

37. How happy are the astrologers! Who believed if they tell one truth to a hundred lies, while other people lose all credit if they tell one lie to a hundred truths! "Marsilio Ficino" (p.528)

Reflection: Usually the soothsayers, the oracles and the fortunetellers have influenced the old rulers and left them with the strongest bewilderment, as they were in the same time happy. Nowadays, the people who are still writing their revelations and telling others about their prophecies are getting credibility

*from decision makers of little learning, for a
little learning is a dangerous thing.*

Philosophy:

38. Wisdom seems always the reincarnation or echo,
since it remains the same through a thousand
varieties and generations of error. (p.539)

*Reflection: As Nifo professed the following
principle: "we must speak as the many do, we
must think as the few." Finally, one can add
to this that we must do as it is appropriate to
us. This becomes the culmination of wisdom
inherited from our forefathers. Our children
will inherit from us the sum of our knowledge
and they will have to do what will be suitable
for them.*

Machiavelli: The Author and the Man:

39. A nation that has lost the martial virtues is
doomed. An army requires not gold but men;"
gold alone will not procure good soldiers, but
good soldiers will always procure gold"; gold

will flow to the strong nation, but strength departs from the rich nation, for wealth makes for ease and decay. (p.552)

Reflection: Leo Tolstoy once said that all is fair *in love and war, but this (all) is still to abide by a certain set of conventional laws. Most importantly, the characters of the warring men are to be unpolluted and focusing only on the war affaires but not on anything that may divert their focus to any other belittled objective. And to do so, a soldier must be extremely fit both mentally and physically. Otherwise, he will easily be distracted by every substantial potential. If he goes averted, and skip the needed focus, he either loses his battle, or loses his respect and dignity even if he wins the battle.*

The Philosopher:

40. Politics he understands as the high art of creating, capturing, protecting, and strengthening a state. (p.555)

Reflection: *Machiavelli, here, wants to insist on the importance of the effect of politics. He argues that politics can even submit the ethics of everything to it. He reasons that there is no metaphysics, no theology, no theism or atheism, no discussion of determination or free will, but is destined to be subordinate to politics or play the role of a tool to politics.*

41. Valor produces peace; peace, repose; repose, disorder; disorder, ruin. From disorder order springs; from order, valor (*virtù*); and from this, glory and good fortune. Hence, wise men have observed that the age of literary excellence is subsequent to that of distinction in arms; and that great warriors are produced before philosophers. (p.556)

Reflection: *It is an inevitable reality to see greenery sprouts from ashes. When wars come and go, next you witness prosperity and progress. There is no escape that one comes after the other.*

42. When a state ceases to expand, it begins to decay; when it loses the will to war, it is finished. Peace too long maintained is enervating and disruptive; an occasional war is a national tonic, restoring discipline, vigor and unity. (p.559)

Reflection: A long period of peace is always followed by a period disturbance. Thus, maintaining the awareness to be ready to war can help shorten the period of war and winning the war. For war is a must, but not a game. It needs to be managed with intelligence and swiftness. Waging wars needs high levels of discipline, and discipline provokes order and progress.

43. Virtue, to a Roman, was not humility, gentleness, or peace, but virility, manliness, courage with energy and intelligence. (p.559)

Reflection: Since virtue is a plus, it can embrace within it all advantages of characters. Virtue cannot mix with negative qualities when it is authentic.

44. A statesman can speak no louder than his guns. (p.562)

Reflection: In our days, guns are not only weaponry; they can be intelligence, charisma, money, connections, authority and knowledge. If these can be used wisely, then a statesman can speak much louder than arms.

45. If a ruler must choose between being feared without love or being loved without fear, he must sacrifice the love. (p. 562)

Reflection: "Love hinders death", as Leo Tolstoy puts it. However, fear can serve a very important purpose for rulers like ours. Our rulers of today strongly believe that being feared rather than being loved can provide them with the safest and shortest way to accomplish their goals. They argue that a frightened and hungry subject is easier to manipulate and easier to submit, because they also consider that hungry bellies never think.

46. Everyone sees what you appear to be, few know what you are; and those few dare not oppose the opinion of the many. (p.563)

Reflection: Rarely are you the one who you appear. To perceive your reality, one needs to spend more time and effort. Rare are the people who dare to pioneer the true self of another person because the majority believe that the reality exists only in the shallowness not in the depth.

BOOK SIX: FINALE
Chapter Twenty-three:
The Waning of the Renaissance

Science and Philosophy:

47. Of all ends that man may attain, none seems more worthy or more pleasing than the recognition of truth. (p.693)

<u>Reflection:</u> Because the recognition of the truth rests on the knowledge of the truth itself, and because the complete knowledge of the truth is nearly impossible, the pleasure that results from the appreciation of the truth is unique in its taste.

Extracted by
Wadih Barakat
for the point of study
30/9/2012

EPILOGUE

Twelve years have passed like a blink as history still passing nearby. Rare are the people who noticed this insatiable hand engraving our rear and front history on the insoluble rock of times.

Will Durant along with his wife Ariel spent effort, time and money to put in our palms, the human race palms, the acumen of the historiology art. This intelligence, if used, we could have spared our race lots of problems. Still we have the opportunities to dodge the coming calamities were we able to read the eleven volumes of *"The Story of Civilizations"* written by them.

In this volume, which is one of a series to come, is the essence of their writings from my own perspective as a reader, a researcher, and an author. Though the goal of extracting from the eleven volumes of Will and

Ariel Durant is a study, still we can use these extracts as **lessons from history** to embellish our future for the sake of our descendants.

Around nine thousand pages were read and thought of to be put into this work.

The author

REFERENCES

The Holy Bible. Printed in Great Britain at the University Press, Oxford by John Johnson War and Peace by Leo Tolstoy, Penguin Classics Dropping Your Guard by Charles R. Swindoll, Word Publishing

Printed in the United States
by Baker & Taylor Publisher Services